Chat
Room
Chatter

Justin

Chat

Room

Chatter

The Buzz on Prom Dates,
Superheroes & the Universe
at Large

Lookadoo

R
Revell
Grand Rapids, Michigan

© 2007 by Justin Lookadoo

Published by Revell
a division of Baker Publishing Group
P.O. Box 6287, Grand Rapids, MI 49516–6287

Printed in the United States of America

    Library of Congress Cataloging-in-Publication Data
Lookadoo, Justin.
        Chat room chatter : the buzz on prom dates,
    superheroes & the universe at large / Justin
    Lookadoo.
            p.   cm.
        ISBN 10: 0-8007-3183-2 (pbk.)
        ISBN 978-0-8007-3183-0 (pbk.)
        1. Christian teenagers—Conduct of life. 2.
    Interpersonal relations—Religious aspects—Chris-
    tianity. 3. Christian teenagers—Religious life. 4.
    Dating (Social customs)—Religious aspects—
    Christianity. I. Title.
    BJ1661.L64 2007
    248.8′3—dc22   2007021756

interior design by Brian Brunsting

Contents

Crushin'

[crushes, true love,
and other matters of the heart]

Subject: RE: #1 How do you know if a guy really likes you?

Date: Monday, June 18, 2007 1:19 PM

From: Live conference

To: 'Justin Lookadoo' <emily@Lookadoo.com>

Conversation: Crushin'

turn this into an article for Ya Mag

He asks you out. Yeah, that should be obvious, but some girls don't even get the hint when that happens.

He starts a convo with you. It takes a lot for a guy to start a conversation with a girl. We are not big talkers in the first place, and then we think we have to have magical words the first time we talk to you. We get butterflies and our bodies and minds go weird. So if the dude talks with you, he likes you.

He teases and makes fun of you. This is old-school playground stuff, but it never changes. If he's teasing you, you're definitely on his radar.

He asks you questions. And he pays attention to the answers. If you happen to tell him what your favorite song is and the next time you see him he has it on his iPod, that's a definite sign.

He locks eyes on you. Guys are visual. So if you catch him looking at you, that's a go. The relational expert people tell us that the first step in a romantic relationship is eye-to-body contact. That means checking each other out.

He wants to spend time with you. He ditches his buds to hang out with you.

He shows off around you. If you see him getting louder and even more obnoxious and doing stupid

1. CALL AL
2. CALL DENNY
3. THANK you to HARRY.
4. Email Mom

stuff around you, that is a sign that he wants you to notice him. "Recognize me! I'm over here." Now, how do you know if that show of testosterone is for you or someone else? Well, has he done any of the other things too? If so, it's for you. If not, it may be for another chick in the flock.

These are a few keepers on how to really know if the guy is really crushing on you. Guys are not that hard to figure out. Just watch what we do and run it through the filter of trying to be cool and trying to get you to like us. Pretty soon you will be an expert on the ploys and efforts of the male species.

jlook

Justin Lookadoo
Check out Justin's bestselling book **Dateable: are you? are they?**

Did you know? The first time Justin bought Emily roses, he bought her two dozen and her mother one . . . and it worked.

Lookadoo

Last Updated:
July 31, 2007

Send Message
Instant Message
Email to a Friend
Subscribe
Invite to My Blog

Gender: Male
Status: Married
Age: 101
Sign: Pisces

City: McKinney
State: TEXAS
Country: US

Signup Date:
02/17/06

Friday, June 02, 2006

#2 How do you know when a girl likes you?

* **She starts showing up wherever you are.** These are usually places that you always go but she has never shown up at before. Now, all of a sudden, there she is.

* **She communicates with you on a regular basis.** That regular basis may just start with a "Hi" every morning and a "How was ball practice?" And then it will gradually get longer.

* **She starts liking stuff that she never liked before.** Prime example: I have a 1972 K5 Chevy Blazer with a six-inch lift, thirty-six-inch tires, a three-ton winch on the front, a brand-new 350 under the hood. Fully convertible, fully restored. Give me a redneck "Yeee-haaaaw!" I love this thing. Well, when Emily and I were dating, we were going to visit my parents two hours away and taking the Blazer. Not a smooth ride but really fun. Emily talked about how much she would love the ride with the top down, and as we drove to the parentals she went on and on about it. Imagine my surprise to learn, now that we are married, that she's not a big fan of riding in the Blazer. But it's not too much of a surprise that she was doing her girl thing by liking stuff that I liked and connecting with me that way. It's cool. I got the girl—and the Blazer.

* **She starts telling you stuff you're really not ready to hear.** This could be secrets, feelings, hopes, future, anything. Girls connect with each other by telling each other stuff. So if she likes you, she will start doing that with you.

* **You catch her looking at you.** Same thing guys do. She is checking you out. It's the whole eye-to-body progression in relationships.

* **Her voice changes.** Girls have a tendency to change their voice while talking with a potential crush. It gets a little softer, a little more feminine.

These are just a few things that may let you know what she is thinking. Relationships and the attraction process are not exact sciences. We can't just whip up a logarithmic formula that will give you the crush factor that leads to success. But these few little tips will help you filter through the confusing messages given by the elusive species we call "female."

9:20 AM - 3 comments - 20 Kudos - Add Comment

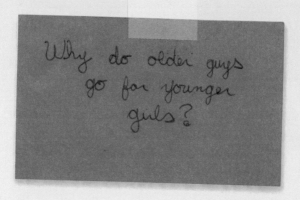

Why do older guys
go for younger
girls?

Okay, what's the question here? Do you want to know why girls *think* older guys go after them, or do you want the truth? Those are totally different answers.

Before we get into the answer, we have to set some parameters here. We are talking about some big age gaps. And the definition of "big" changes. Check it: A three-year gap is huge when she is 13 and he is 16. But a thirteen-year gap is nothing when she is 60 and he is 73. When you are in high school and you are more than two years apart, then it's a major difference in where you are in life.

Younger girls *think* the reason older guys go after them is because they are obviously more mature. So far beyond all the other girls. And girls, this may be true. You may be very mature for your age (just like every other girl). But that really has nothing to do with why older guys go after younger girls.

Most of the time when this older guy/younger girl thing happens, it has very little to do with *her* maturity. It has a lot more to do with *his* immaturity. He can't relate to girls his own age, and they won't let him get away with the crap that younger girls do.

Oh, I know, if you are that girl, you don't let him get away with anything. Listen, a lot of stuff happens that you don't know is happening because you haven't gone through it. You haven't experienced certain things, so you don't know how to recognize them when they're happening. You haven't watched this dude as long as girls his age have. So if he's not with girls his age, it's because they see something that you don't, and they are more than happy to kick him to you.

Also, younger girls often get caught up in "an older guy likes me" syndrome. And so you overlook a lot of what goes on. You let him say stuff about you, or maybe let his hands wander too far. Maybe you cut out all your friends while he still hangs out with his. Or it could be that you have to check in with him all the time and he goes places and doesn't offer you any details of where and who he will be with. I don't know, I am just throwing out some possibilities of how younger girls get caught up in dating an older guy. It's okay. You don't have to admit it if you don't want to. But a lot of you reading this right now know what I'm talking about.

Another reason that older guys start creeping up on younger girls is because younger girls are easier. They may put up a bigger front at first, but younger girls can be led into sexual stuff pretty easily. It just takes the dude getting her to feel like he loves her as much as she loves him, and even that's not seriously difficult.

So girls, I'm sure you don't like my answer, but hey, I'm okay with that. As long as you understand that it doesn't have to be this way. When these older guys start chasing you, now you can take control. You can be flattered that he made the effort, but you now understand what is really happening, so you get to keep yourself strong and confident and let him know that it's not going to work. At least not with you.

Kinda stuck on Himself eh?

Tue, July 31, 2007 9:18 PM

Subject: RE: #4 What can you do when a girl is stalking you?
Date: Tuesday, May 1, 2007 9:49 PM
From: Live conference
To: 'Justin Lookadoo' <emily@Lookadoo.com>
Conversation: Crushin'

Okay, if she is stalking you in an I'm-going-to-boil-your-bunny-rabbit-alive-if-you-don't-love-me kinda way, then you need to call the police and get a restraining order.

If it is one of those things where she seems to always follow you around and she is always bugging you and won't leave you alone, then you are totally responsible for how you treat her.

I'll break it down for you a little bit. Quick question: this girl who won't seem to leave you alone—what if she was hot? Would you be bugged out about it, or would you be telling everybody that the hot girl was after you? Hey, you don't have to be ashamed of the answer. I'd be the same way. So the real deal is *not* that the girl is annoying and stalking you. It's that a girl you don't think is hot is all over you. And hey, that's cool. But you have to first admit that we are dealing with your ego and not really the stalking stuff.

Ain't that the truth!

You can sit there and say, "No, you're wrong. That's not it." Yeah, okay. How do you think I knew to ask if she was hot? Easy. It's happened to me before. And the only times I got all upset about a girl being way too pushy was when it was one I didn't want to go out with. So if you can accept that what I am say-

Who is going to argue with this the most
❋ Good - Nice ❋
❋ guys. ❋   Bad-Boys

I REMEMBER the guy who ASKED this. He was nice But he was Also the 'cool' guy.

ing has some truth to it, then we can do something about it.

Starting point: this girl is a princess. Even if you don't think she is beautiful, God does. She is a precious creation of a powerful Creator. Read that again. She is a precious creation of a powerful Creator. One more time. She is a precious creation of a powerful Creator. Keep reading that until you believe it. This is where you start.

Let's just run through some scenarios and we'll check out a few things you can do when this girl starts getting a little pushy.

Her Deal: She asks you a lot of questions.

Your Deal: Answer them. That is just being polite. Remember, if she was hot or even just someone else, you would probably answer them. So do it now.

Her Deal: She's always where you are.

Your Deal: Just keep doing whatever you normally do. This is not a big deal. We make it a big deal in our heads.

Her Deal: She shows up to your ball game with your face on her T-shirt and a megaphone.

Your Deal: Yeah, this one is a **code red.** Something has to be done. Here's how you handle it. Whenever you can get to her—not where the world can hear, just her—tell her the truth. Something like this: "The shirt and the megaphone really embarrassed me, and in fact it embarrassed me so much that I couldn't even play the game." Remember, she likes you, and she wouldn't want you to be upset or em-

This won't be the last time this happens to Him

barrassed. You need to have the same consideration for her when you tell her this. Don't do it in front of everyone. Don't embarrass her. And don't yak about it with your friends either. She'll be crushed, and you'll look like a jerk. And if you want to get all biblical about it, check out Matthew 25:40: "I tell you the truth, whatever you did for one of the least of these brothers of mine, you did for me." You know what I'm saying. She is the last one on your list. <u>The least.</u> So however you treat her, that's how you are treating Christ. You're not doing it to her; you're doing it to him.

Advanced Advice: Don't tell her that you don't want to go out with her unless she pushes the point. She may not have romance on the mind. It may be that you are just one of the only people to be nice to her. If you throw the date block out there before the question comes up, then you are a conceited jerk who thinks everyone who talks to you wants to go out with you. Not a good deal.

There was this girl in college who always seemed to be a little too close and clingy. She was the nicest girl in the world. She would do anything to help anyone, especially me. She was a little awkward and didn't have a ton of friends. I was nice to her like I am with everyone, and she latched on to me.

One day she came up to where I was sitting and handed me a letter that she had written for me. She sat down and waited for me to read it. In it she poured out her feelings for me, and as I read it I knew she was expecting a response.

A little Awkward → Alot!

I stared at the paper an extra long time, trying to find something to say.

I folded up the paper. I looked her in the eye (that is important) and said, "Wow. How flattering. It's an honor to know how you feel. However, the relationship we have now will not transform into a romantic one."

She cried and said that she was embarrassed. I told her not to be embarrassed and that I respected her for telling me. She told me that she didn't think we would be able to be as close of friends as we used to be. I told her I understood.

As she started to leave she asked if she could have one last hug. It was a little awkward, but I gave her a hug and she left. (If you really don't want to go there with a hug, then simply say, "I really don't feel comfortable with that. I'm sure you understand.")

And guess what? All of the "stalking" behavior stopped. It was on her terms. I wasn't mean, and I sure didn't jump the gun and shoot her down before she even brought it up. Now if I see her out and about, neither one of us has regrets, and we can talk knowing that I wasn't rude or a jerk.

jlook

Did you know? Justin has an older sister named Michelle who has a monogramming business named Lookadoodles.

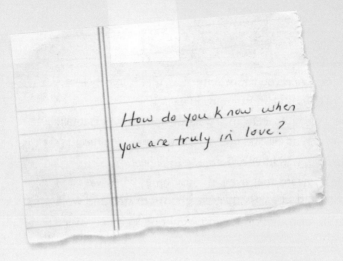

How do you know when you are truly in love?

When people think of love, they think of this gushy feel-good vibe they get when they are with a certain person. Or the way they miss them when they are apart. That's not love. Those are mushy-gushy feelings and nothing more.

Now don't get me wrong. Those zingers that shoot through you and make you start feeling all weird inside, they are cool feelings—but they are *not* love.

Love is a choice. Love is saying that I am with you till the end. No matter how good or how bad it gets, I am with you and I'm not going anywhere. I will be with you forever or die trying my best to make it happen. In fact, that's exactly what 1 John 3:16 says about love: "This is how we know what love is: Jesus Christ laid down his life for us. And we ought to lay down our lives for our brothers." I will put down my life, desires, and selfishness so they won't destroy my love.

Emily and I totally enjoy the butterfly kind of feelings that we get sometimes. But that doesn't happen all the time. If that was what we considered love, we wouldn't be in love very much. But love is waking up every day and saying, "I choose you." And you know, some days that is so easy to do, and some days it's almost impossible.

There are days that Em and I wake up and we are still totally ticked at each other. She rolls over and thinks, *Bummer, he's still breathing.* And I think, *Darn, she's still here.*

But love means that even in those times when we can't stand the sight of each other, we choose to stay and work through it, even though leaving would be so much easier. That's love.

Let me tell you this, though. If you are dating someone and most of the time you seem to have to work through lots of issues with lots of arguments, and if you spend more time having to choose to be in the relationship than wanting to be in it, then you are not in love. You are desperate. You need to get some guts, figure out that you do not have to be in a relationship to feel loved and important, and move on.

For a final note on what love really is, check out 1 Corinthians 13:4–6 and it will give you the goods:

> Love is patient, love is kind. It does not envy, it does not boast, it is not proud. It is not rude, it is not self-seeking, it is not easily angered, it keeps no record of wrongs. Love does not delight in evil but rejoices with the truth. It always protects, always trusts, always hopes, always perseveres.

Think about every word of that passage to see if you are really in love.

Patient—Doesn't expect the other person to call all the time. Or to be perfect. And is willing to wait forever for God to work on them.

Kind—Not just to each other but to everyone else too.

Not Jealous—Thinks about your own actions, making sure nothing would give the other person a reason to get jealous.

Doesn't Boast—Not always focused on how good they are.

Isn't Rude—Doesn't say mean, rude things. Doesn't do things that are rude—and that means to the person or to others.

And definitely look at the last part. Love *always* protects, *always* trusts, *always* hopes, *always* perseveres. Not just when things are happy and beautiful. In every situation. Even when your anger or actions are deserved.

Do what this says. And that is love.

Did you know Justin has a biology degree focused on premed. Even with all that chemistry, he still didn't know

$$2 \times (C_4H_{10}(g) + 6\ 1/2O_2(g) \longrightarrow 4CO_2(g) + 5H_2O(l))$$

Monday, April 2, 2007

#6 Why do girls look for lean/muscular guys who are horrible in relationships?

Why? The same reason guys look for fit/fine girls who may or may not be horrible in relationships. In your question your focus is on why girls "look" for guys. The first part in the attraction process is eye-to-body contact. That means you are checking the person out. You don't know if they are good or bad in relationships; you are just checking them out.

Now, let's get down to some issues. When someone asks a question, they always have a reason. Maybe you were liking someone but you got blocked by someone who was good-looking, and now you are looking for a way to justify it to yourself, because obviously it couldn't have been because the person just didn't like you like that. Or maybe you really don't like the way you look and that totally translates to other people. Hey, if you think you're not attractive, do something to make yourself like the way you look. It may be losing weight, brushing your hair, ironing your clothes—hey, I can't see you, so I am just throwing out options. But let me tell you this. If the person you're crushing on looks at you and you don't take care of yourself, down deep in the subconscious mind they will automatically connect the dots: "If they don't take care of themselves, then they sure can't take care of me." It's automatic.

That doesn't mean you have to get some nip and tuck magic to make you look beautiful. It does mean that you have to care about who you are. Be confident and understand that it's true, "Beauty is in the eye of the beholder." That just means if you are solid in how you feel about you, then your attractiveness will show.

10:26 AM - **8 comments** - **3 Kudos** - **Add Comment**

how old are they?

Subject: RE: #7 If I don't feel that *zazazu* passion thing, is our relationship okay?
Date: Thursday, January 11, 2007 12:37 PM
From: Live conference
To: 'Justin Lookadoo' <emily@Lookadoo.com>
Conversation: Crushin'

Romance?
· Massage
· Bath
· Out
· Cruise

After years and years and years of marriage, okay, maybe. But in the beginning, no. That is the spice in the relationship. That is the stuff that makes your heart jump when they look at you. That's the romance. You may not think it's important now, but give it a few years and you will want to feel what fairy tales are made of. You will need someone to make you feel like that, and you will eventually meet someone who will.

Now let me throw this out there. That electric charge is something that will come and go. You don't have to feel it every minute of every second. It's just a part of the relationship. If you do feel it and that's the foundation of your togetherness, then you are going to crash and burn. Most days you won't feel it that strong. Your relationship has to be built on being with someone you can count on. Your best friend. The two of you doing life together. Marriage isn't all horse-drawn carriages and all-night sexfests. So you have to have a balance.

Yeah, I wish!

jlook

Justin Lookadoo
Buy Justin's hit new release **97**

Tonight: Make a list of Romance Ideas.

Subject: RE: #8 How do you let it go when you took a girl too seriously and got hurt?
Date: Wednesday, December 27, 2006 1:12 AM
From: Live conference
To: 'Justin Lookadoo' <emily@Lookadoo.com>
Conversation: Crushin'

You won't believe you'll get over it until you do. Right now everything in your life is intensified. A lot of the things you are into are firsts for you. First crush. First serious gf. First time to feel that connected. Your first driver's license, first car, first job. Everything is amped up and accelerated because it's fresh and new.

Then you add a bunch of hormones into your mix and everything goes nuclear. You don't just get a pimple; you get a small planet attached to your face. One fight with your parents makes you want to crawl away and hide. You get angry more. Depressed more. Everything escalates with hormones. You feel on fire for life and still out of control.

Yeah, I know that's not the answer to your question, but you need to know that right now things seem hyperintense because of the newness and because hormones are totally twisting the way you see, feel, and react to things.

Now, to get over the fact that you got way too serious about this relationship, well, the answer is time. You will feel it until you don't. I know, stupid answer, but it's the truth. Right now you have an open wound, and just like a physical wound, it will take time to heal. In the meantime, go play ball. Hike. Go to the movies. Whatever you normally like to do, get

[Handwritten in left margin: Muy importante]

deeper into it. Try spending some time writing in a journal or praying or walking around seeing what God wants to show you.

As you heal and move past this relationship, please don't make a fool of yourself in the process. Don't talk to the person. This will only open up the wound. Don't take them back. Don't do or say anything that you could regret. You will be able to let go as the distance builds and time passes. And next time hopefully you will remember the painful lesson of giving too much too quick.

jlook

Justin Lookadoo
Order your copy of the
3-part Dateable DVD *now!* *product@lookadoo.com*

[Handwritten: This is where most regret comes from in the breakup/healing process]

Monday, October 16, 2006

#9 How do I get over a guy? I have a new boyfriend now, but I just can't get over my ex.

You need to forgive yourself for going too far. You gave too much. Either physically or emotionally, you let that ex have way too much, and it created an unhealthy connection between you.

That's why it is so important to control what and how much you give to a relationship before you are married. You are putting all of you into a relationship that really is not yours yet. Without a true commitment between you and God, you know, that thing called marriage, you are investing in a relationship that isn't 100% connected to you. That is a bad investment to make.

After you forgive yourself, the goal is to not go through the same thing with your next bf. If you get too physical or too emotional in this relationship and then this one ends, well, guess what will happen with the next guy. You will have trouble getting over the last *two*. Protect your connections. You don't want to have a bunch of people connected to you dragging you down.

7:48 PM - **8 comments** - **9 Kudos** - **Add Comment**

26

Lookadoo

Last Updated:
July 31, 2007

Send Message
Instant Message
Email to a Friend
Subscribe
Invite to My Blog

Gender: Male
Status: Married
Age: 101
Sign: Pisces

City: McKinney
State: TEXAS
Country: US

Signup Date:
02/17/06

Saturday, January 6, 2007

#10 Is it wrong to set high standards for a guy? Your friends will say you are too picky, and guys will say you think you are too good.

You are not wrong! Girls, listen to me: you are not wrong to set high standards. Never, ever lower yourself so that a guy feels like he is more of a man. Make a guy step up and do what he has to do to be a man.

But here's the deal: you are not obligated to share your standards with anyone. In fact, I encourage you not to. If you tell all your girl friends about your standards, then you give them reasons to attack you for your beliefs. And you are right; the reason they rip on you is because they are not doing it. As for the guys, don't let them know what your standards are because that gives the dude clues on how to get you. See, guys love the game. They love the chase. If you tell them how to get you, they will fake it long enough to get you. That doesn't mean he has changed; it just means he's playing the relationship game.

Not sharing your standards doesn't mean you are hiding your beliefs. If you live what you believe in every area of your life, then people really won't question your decisions. They will know that you are consistent, you are confident, and your life is full because of your relationship with Christ, and they won't need to speculate. Sure, you may still find some who trash you, but it will be for different reasons—for the girls, because they want what you have, and for the guys, because they are not man enough to get you. Accept this as a trophy every time it happens. It is proof that people can see your life as an example of Christ.

Consider it pure joy, my brothers, whenever you face trials of many kinds. —James 1:2

8:13 AM - 6 comments - 2 Kudos - Add Comment

Subject: RE: #11 Should we look for a man who can spiritually lead us or grow with us?
Date: Thursday, February 8, 2007 11:49 AM
From: Live conference
To: 'Justin Lookadoo' <emily@Lookadoo.com>
Conversation: Crushin'

Yes. Ephesians 5:23 says, "For the husband is the head of the wife as Christ is the head of the church." That means the man should lead her and be the one she can follow and count on to guide and protect her. But he also has to be growing with her. If he isn't growing, then the relationship will be stagnant. And if you aren't moving forward, you are sliding backwards. Sitting still is not an option.

So the answer is yes. You want a guy who will lead you spiritually *and* also grow with you.

jlook

Justin Lookadoo
See what is happening at www.Lookadoo.com

College = Adult

Go into the stuff about times when (HE) is leading it & times when (SHE) is. THIS is A TEAM EFFORT.

also, try the umbrella stuff

Talk to Emily ABOUT Submission stuff.

Lookadoo

Last Updated:
July 31, 2007

Send Message
Instant Message
Email to a Friend
Subscribe
Invite to My Blog

Gender: Male
Status: Married
Age: 101
Sign: Pisces

City: McKinney
State: TEXAS
Country: US

Signup Date:
02/17/06

Friday, February 23, 2007

#12 I like this girl and I know she likes me. I asked her out and she said yes, but then a few days later she said no because her parents didn't approve. What should I do?

Walk away! It sucks to be you right now, but that is a bad deal to get into. If you bully through it the relationship will be built on defiance, rebellion, and deceit. The attraction and excitement will come from giving the parents a big "screw you." If they finally quit fighting the relationship, the two of you will break up because the foundational attraction is no longer there. If the drama continues, you will end up splitting because you'll get tired of not having a relationship—because all you'll have is a struggle. If, for some reason, you were to go out and get married, it would be a long, hard trip. You would constantly feel the pressure and strain of family problems.

Relationships are tough. Don't make them tougher by jumping into a relationship that the parents disapprove of and will do what they can to destroy. This relationship will be fueled by a rebellious spirit. And that won't last.

2:37 PM - 5 comments - 13 Kudos - Add Comment

Tuesday, March 27, 2007

#13 What if you start liking your best friend's bf/gf? Should you go ahead and pursue it?

Absolutely not! There is no good ending possible in that.

If you go after your friend's crush, you could end up getting them. This relationship will be built on deceit and selfishness. It will end, and it will probably end by the person moving on to one of your friends. Then you end up with an ex-crush and an ex–best friend.

Or, in the best case scenario, you could make your move and have it not work, and then you have totally destroyed your friendship. I know that's not a great answer either, but I told you there are no good answers.

The answer you want—you know, where you go after your crush and win them over while your best friend, while sad, understands your love for each other and so helps you in your quest and helps plan your wedding . . . yeah, that one doesn't exist.

Oh, and don't think your friendship is big enough to survive the crush double-cross. It's not. Even if they say they don't mind, they do. Wouldn't you?

Now, with all of that said and with you knowing that you have these feelings, you have to take major precautions. You cannot be alone with your friend's crush. Do not share secrets with them; do not go places with them. Why? Because the next email I get will be from you saying that you were out this weekend and you accidentally kissed your best friend's bf/gf. Neither of you planned it or wanted it to happen, it just happened, and now you don't know what to do because you don't want to lose your best friend. Hey, if you choose to ignore what I'm telling you, then do not contact me with your mess-up. I warned you.

3:05 PM - 15 comments - 4 Kudos - Add Comment

Subject: RE: #14 Is it okay to flirt with stuffed animals?

Date: Saturday, August 5, 2006 9:01 AM

From: Live conference

To: 'Justin Lookadoo' <emily@Lookadoo.com>

Conversation: Crushin'

Yes. It's a little weird, but it's perfectly normal. I did. Well, that's not a good guide for normal. But I even kissed my stuffed animals. I know—I need help.

jlook

Justin Lookadoo
Buy Justin's hit new release **97**

Go to the Storage Building & see if I still have mine!

There were two. Brown Bear & A Pooh Bear kind of Thing. Brown Bear was the Main one!

It would Be fun to HAVE these on stage

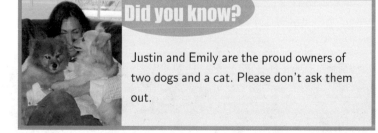

Did you know?

Justin and Emily are the proud owners of two dogs and a cat. Please don't ask them out.

Is it okay to lust over cartoon characters?

Yes. I mean, no. I mean, okay, here's what I mean: cartoon characters are drawn really hot. And they can be totally enhanced so that they are even hotter than any real person ever could be. So in that way you're not a weirdo for checking out the cartoon hottie.

However, lust is lust. It doesn't matter if it's lusting over a girl, a cartoon, a chair, or anything else. Lust is a sin that cuts your connection with God. So in that way it's wrong.

So to think a cartoon girl is hot, that's cool. To go further than that into running a little touchy-feely free-for-all in your mind, that's sin.

Lookadoo

Last Updated:
July 31, 2007

Send Message
Instant Message
Email to a Friend
Subscribe
Invite to My Blog

Gender: Male
Status: Married
Age: 101
Sign: Pisces

City: McKinney
State: TEXAS
Country: US

Signup Date:
02/17/06

Thursday, June 7, 2007

#16 I'm a girl who isn't going to kiss until my wedding day. If all guys want is sex, how am I supposed to get a guy?

Ah, but guys love a challenge. We love the chase. And if you hold off on anything, then you become the prize. The trophy. If you become stronger and more attractive on every level—mentally, spiritually, emotionally, socially, and physically—and you do not give out your intimacy, then you will become like that jewel that is wanted by all.

Here's what will be the tough part for you. You will be like that perfect diamond. Beautiful. Rare. The one everyone would love to have. But most guys won't even try because they know that you, like that diamond, are so far out of their reach, and they'll think, *Why bother?* But stay strong and confident. There will be someone who will want that diamond enough to work for it. Same thing's true for you. The perfect person will come along and do whatever it takes to win your love.

1:12 PM - **6 comments** - **2 Kudos** - **Add Comment**

Do you think there is one perfect person out there for every person?

No, and here's why. If there is just one perfect person out there for each person, what if I mess up and marry the person my friend was supposed to marry? That means he would have to take someone else's perfect person because I took his. Then that person would have to take someone else's, and then the whole system is jacked up.

I think that God has made us suited to be with different people. And our age and where we are in our lives will shape who we choose as our perfect person.

Did you know Justin and Emily got engaged in Sedona, Arizona.

Prom Dates

[dating and relationship stuff]

Did you KNOW?

If you have heard Justin speak, you know about his baby, this 1972 K5 Blazer—6-inch lift, 36-inch tire, 3-ton winch, brand-new vortex 350, fully convertible, and full of fun. What you may not know is that his wife, Emily, decided to sneak it out and take it for a joy ride. She ran it through their house. Justin is still bitter and they are still married.

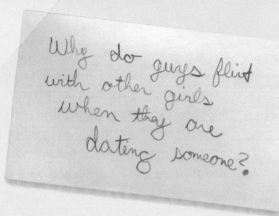
Why do guys flirt with other girls when they are dating someone?

If you ask the guy, he'll probably tell you that he's just being nice. Or that it's just the way he is and it doesn't mean anything. If you want the truth, I'll give it to you.

1. It's an *ego boost.* A guy wants to know that he has a girl, and then he wants to feel like he can get any other girl.

2. The guy may be *testing the waters.* He is putting the relationship to the test. He is wanting to make sure that the two of you have the best connection. And what better way to do that than to flirt with other people? He proves to himself that the feelings he has for you are stronger than any he could have with another. Yeah, I know, that's some really jacked-up logic, but it's true.

   Now the problem with this theory is that given the right day where you guys have not been getting along the best and the right girl in the right moment, he will find a chemical flare set off by another hottie, and he'll decide to move on.

3. It may be nothing more than him *getting comfortable.* When you really get to know someone, some of the

edginess of getting to know each other is replaced with the comfort of knowing. But when you're flirting with someone new, that edge is there. It's exciting and fun. A lot of couples head for trouble at this point because they find the next exciting thing and never feel the power and beauty of getting to know someone deeply.

4. And finally, there is always the classic of *wanting to know that you get jealous.* If you don't get jealous, then the dude doesn't think you like him very much. Like one dude put it, "I want to know that it bothers her."

Hey, you asked the question why. Here are some of the biggest reasons for dating one and flirting with the others. There are no good answers here. If your fella is doing it, you really need to evaluate your relationship, because it is in a serious danger zone.

Subject: RE: #19 Why do girls flirt with other guys when they are going out with someone?

Date: Sunday, August 6, 2006 5:21 PM

From: Live conference

To: 'Justin Lookadoo' <emily@Lookadoo.com>

Conversation: Prom Dates

Girls flirt while in a relationship for many of the same reasons guys do. But a major difference for the flirtatious female is that she always wants to know that she's hot, that everyone notices her. This flows into everything: the way she dresses, the makeup she wears, the way she flirts, where she stands, everything.

If you really look at it, she's really not that interested in hooking the guy. She is really competing with the other girls. Hey, she may not feel totally beautiful—most girls don't—but she wants to feel like she is more attractive than any of the other girls around at the moment.

Let me tell you the real deal from the land of Lookadoo. Flirting can be fun. It's a rush. It's exciting. But if you are in a relationship, seemingly harmless flirting will destroy it. In fact, I love to flirt, and so does my wife. But we have to make a very deliberate choice to basically be boring around someone of the opposite sex. Because there is nothing healthy about flirting when you are hooked up with someone. Jealousy is not good. You don't put yourself in a situation that will make the other person question. You don't disrespect them by flirting with others, and you totally understand that at the right time in the right moment under the right circumstances, you will always find someone more exciting than the person you are with. That doesn't mean you are in a bad relationship. That just means you are not at the strongest point of the relationship, and that weakness mixed with harmless flirting can kill your relationship. In fact, Song of Solomon warns about this several times with the exact same phrase: "Do not arouse or awaken love until it so desires" (see chapter 2 verse 7, for example). That's exactly what flirting is trying to do. It is trying to get a reaction, to make the other person feel a hint of desire or love or even like towards you. Do not try to wake up that beast, because once it's awake, you can't just ignore it.

jlook

Justin Lookadoo
Order your copy of the
3-part Dateable DVD now! *product@lookadoo.com*

[handwritten: Get MORE verses that to Relate this!]

[handwritten: Q: Why do you flirt? [Fun] : Why is it fun? : What do you get from it? (Get down to the Root)]

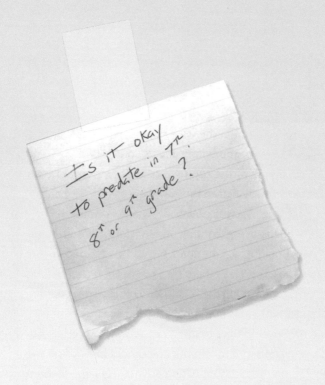

Is it okay
to predate in 7th.
8th or 9th grade?

Uh . . . I have no idea what that means, so NO!

Yes. But probably not in the way you are thinking.

Feeling too fat or too skinny affects your confidence, and confidence is one of the top factors in attraction. And our confidence is totally tied to the way we feel, our self-control, and our ability to do what we want when we want.

If someone is overweight or underweight—not as determined by a height/weight chart but as determined by the way they look and feel—there's a reason. Eating the wrong amounts of food. Eating the wrong kinds of food. Not getting exercise. Something is not in balance and control.

God made our bodies to run a certain way on certain nutrients. And I have got to tell you, you cannot be 5 foot 4 and weigh 250 pounds without eating an insanely large amount of food. On the flip side, you cannot be 5 foot 6 and weigh 98 pounds without eating an insanely small amount of food. Either way it goes, this will affect the way you feel physically. This will influence the way you look at yourself, and it will impact your relationships.

So what can you do? Get control of your life. Figure out what triggers your eating style. Most overly large people eat when they are stressed, upset, or bored. Most overly skinny people will skip meals for the same reasons. Figuring out your pattern is the first step. In fact, write it down. Here, I'll make steps for you to follow.

1. Figure out your eating pattern.

2. Drink water. Start with four 8-ounce glasses a day and then work your way up to a gallon a day. I have a gallon jug that I drink every day. Emily has a bottle that she has to refill four times to make a gallon. Just keep track because you won't do it if you just guess.

3. Keep a little tablet or note cards or something with you and write down everything you eat, when you eat, and how much you eat for three days. This is the amount of sodas, cheese, everything.

4. Start doing something physical. Walk, play ball, do sit-ups, lift weights. Start doing anything for 20 minutes per day for three days each week. You gotta start ramping this up.

5. Take your food log to a trainer, or a counselor at school, or a youth pastor, or the YMCA, or even your local gym. Tell them that you feel lousy, tired, or whatever, and tell them you want to change. Many gyms and youth organizations have discounts or even free facilities for teens. Do whatever they set up for you to do, and take control of your life.

Did you know Justin's family raised goats. One of them is 6'7".

I guarantee that if you do this, your weight won't be an issue. Not because you turned into some Greek god in two weeks. But this will totally change the way you feel, and your confidence will get kicked into overdrive. Go make it happen.

Here are a few other hints for getting your best body:

1. Cut out fast food. All of it!

2. Eat lots of grilled chicken and vegetables.

3. Eat breakfast! Unhealthy people skip breakfast. And don't eat donuts and OJ either. More like a few egg whites, some oatmeal, and fruit.

4. Drink lots of water. A gallon a day.

This isn't new stuff. Healthy food makes a healthy person. You may remember hearing about Daniel and a few of his friends named Shadrach, Meshach, and Abednego. They were in the king's training program, and part of the deal was they got all of this tasty, not-so-great-for-you food and wine straight from the king's table. These guys knew what it would do to their bodies, and they also knew God told them not to eat it. So they made a deal with the head trainer. A ten-day test. If they could only have fresh vegetables and water, then they would be tested against everyone else to make sure they weren't suffering by not eating all the rich food. Pick the story up in verse 14 of Daniel 1: "So he agreed to this and tested them for ten days. At the end of the ten days they looked healthier and better nourished than any of the young men who ate the royal food. So the guard took away their choice food and the wine they were to drink and gave them vegetables instead" (verses 14–16).

What you put in will determine the kind of person you will be. And I don't think it's a coincidence that we see in verse 17 it says, "To these four young men God gave knowledge and understanding of all kinds of literature and learning." I really think there is supposed to be a connection between the food we eat and our mental abilities. Hmmm. Interesting.

Did you know Emily drinks two gallons of water each day. She gets 8 refills to make two gallons.

Subject: RE: #22 What do Christian guys and girls need from a good, healthy relationship?
Date: Saturday, September 16, 2006 3:33 PM
From: Live conference
To: 'Justin Lookadoo' <emily@Lookadoo.com>
Conversation: Prom Dates

→ from you!

Girls, here's what a guy needs: be desirable. Before marriage be a challenge. Keep him chasing. After marriage he needs sex. Inspire him and let him know you need him. Make your guy rise to the occasion of coming after you without pressuring him to do it. A guy will do just about anything if he knows that you need him, want him, and choose him. Be confident in who you are, and give him a role in your life. Don't be overly independent.

Fellas, a girl needs to know that she can follow you—that you are going somewhere and you have what it takes to lead her there. She needs to know that you will be faithful forever. She needs safety, and that means knowing you'll never leave. She needs to know that her needs come first. That means if you are cold and she is hot, then you turn on the A/C and you sleep in your coat. She needs to know that she is the prettiest girl in the room. It doesn't matter if there are a thousand people or just the two of you. She needs to see you looking at her and your eyes not roaming. She needs to know that you are totally committed to God and his will. Then she will know that you are committed to marriage, and she will follow you anywhere.

jlook

LEARN to out GIVE EACH OTHER.

Lookadoo

Last Updated:
July 31, 2007

Send Message
Instant Message
Email to a Friend
Subscribe
Invite to My Blog

Gender: Male
Status: Married
Age: 101
Sign: Pisces

City: McKinney
State: TEXAS
Country: US

Signup Date:
02/17/06

Wednesday, March 21, 2007

#23 My last relationship was abusive, but I got out of it. My boyfriend now would never hurt me, but sometimes when he touches me I get really weird about it. What can I do to get past it?

First of all, you are not weird. You're normal. It doesn't matter if it was physical abuse where you were hit, slapped, or pushed or emotional abuse where you were constantly torn down and told how horrible and ugly you were—abuse is abuse. And you getting all weird is a normal reaction that means your body and mind are trying to protect you. In fact, it proves you are normal.

Moving forward will take time. I know, that's not the magic pill you were hoping to swallow, but you have to get your confidence and security back. And the way you do this is by spending time with safe, comforting males that you feel secure being around. That way your mind and body can get out of that crisis mode. You have to let yourself experience the truth that not everyone is abusive and that you are okay.

You deserve more. Even if someone has convinced you that you don't, you do. God made you to be a princess. The enemy, Satan, knows that. He will use your abuse to try to convince you that you are worthless. That is not the truth! Here's the truth: it's not your fault. Nothing you did made him abuse you. You were not too irritating, ugly, stupid, or anything else he told you. Don't abuse yourself by wondering what *you* did wrong. *He* is the one with the issues. You are okay. You are okay. You are okay.

You need to watch out for another issue if you were abused while growing up or have had abusive boyfriends. Sometimes your mind connects abuse with love. I know it sounds crazy, but our minds don't always make sense. And what could happen is that when you start finding yourself in good relationships, you start getting weird and sabotaging them. So much so that you break up for no real reason because something just doesn't seem right. That's your faulty mind making a connection that abuse equals love—"So if he doesn't abuse me, he must not love me." Logically, it doesn't make sense. But for the girls who read this and think it makes total sense, I urge you to talk with someone about it. A counselor, a therapist, a pastor, anyone. Tell them about the abuse and that you really think you are sabotaging good relationships now. Let them help you.

One more little Lookadoo thought before we go: girls, if you get into a relationship and he is aggressive or abusive either physically or emotionally, get out and get out now. It will *NOT* get any better. And if you don't believe me, believe every abused girl who was in the same situation and kept hanging on hoping it would get better. Remember, you've been in this relationship a month, three months, six months, maybe a year. You are still in the "honeymoon" phase. That means he is still trying to impress you. Imagine what it will be like when he's not trying to impress you. Things won't magically get better.

And for the guys: if you ever start telling girls that they are worthless or ugly or you ever hit them or get physically aggressive with them, you need to get some help. You have some major issues. And you know, I hope you have good enough friends that they won't just let you get away with it but will beat the fool out of you. [Note: For legal reasons we cannot condone or endorse the use of any form of violence against another person no matter how stupid they are.] And I hope her father finds out and he handles it like a true man of God—with the grace and forgiveness of the New Testament and the wrath and vengeance of the Old Testament. Enough said.

11:57 PM - **13 comments** - **6 Kudos** - **Add Comment**

Subject: RE: #24 I've forgiven myself for my past, but how can I forgive my bf or gf for their past?
Date: Saturday, October 1, 2006 10:09 AM
From: Live conference
To: 'Justin Lookadoo' <emily@Lookadoo.com>
Conversation: Prom Dates

FORGIVENESS

It's not really your deal to forgive them. Forgiveness is between them and God. Your deal is getting through your hang-up about their past. It's more of a grace issue than forgiveness. You need to really understand the grace God gave you. Your bf/gf's past was not a sin against you. It was a sin against a holy Creator, the same as yours was. He is the forgiver.

GRACE!

For you to move past this, focus on grace. Every time you think you can't get past *their* past, remember the grace that you've been given.

> For all have sinned and fall short of the glory of God, and are justified freely by his (grace) through the redemption that came by Christ Jesus.
>
> Romans 3:23-24

> For if the many died by the trespass of the one man, how much more did God's (grace) and the gift that came by the (grace) of the one man, Jesus Christ, overflow to the many!
>
> Romans 5:15

> But where sin increased, (grace) increased all the more.
>
> Romans 5:20

Refocus on the REAL focus!

For by the (grace) given me I say to every one of you: Do not think of yourself more highly than you ought, but rather think of yourself with sober judgment, in accordance with the measure of faith God has given you.

Romans 12:3

And God is able to make all (grace) abound to you, so that in all things at all times, having all that you need, you will abound in every good work.

2 Corinthians 9:8

I could keep going, but I think you might get the hint. I'll leave you with one last thought:

(Grace) to all who love our Lord Jesus Christ with an undying love.

Ephesians 6:24

Now, sometimes the fact that you can't get over someone's past is an internal sign that you should get out of the relationship. Maybe it's a check that you have been given to make you think twice about this connection.

jlook

- -

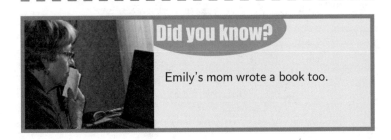

Did you know?

Emily's mom wrote a book too.

Lookadoo

Last Updated:
July 31, 2007

Send Message
Instant Message
Email to a Friend
Subscribe
Invite to My Blog

Gender: Male
Status: Married
Age: 101
Sign: Pisces

City: McKinney
State: TEXAS
Country: US

Signup Date:
02/17/06

Tuesday, February 6, 2007

#25 What would you do if someone asked you out, then stopped talking to you, then decided to make you look like a fool over a 3-way telephone setup?

I would never say another word to the person. But I have to tell you something: the crush that crushed you is not the biggest issue. What you said *is*. I guess this would be a good time to remind you of something in the Bible. Proverbs 20:3 of the Good News Translation says, "Any fool can start arguments; the honorable thing is to stay out of them."

There are ways to say things without being mean. Instead of calling someone an idiot or a jerk for what they did, you can say something like "My feelings get hurt when they do _____" or "It upsets me when they say _____."

Yeah, that is a much better approach.

If you ever do get caught up in this kind of triangle and you say things that you regret or feel sorry for, then don't blame the person who set you up. Own what you did, and tell the person that you were wrong to say what you said and you are sorry. It may not make things better, but it's what you have to do, and maybe you will learn something out of the deal.

Growing up and maturing is about self-censorship. It's about understanding that there is a time and a place for everything and that you are responsible for every word that comes out of your mouth. So no matter what you are saying, always pretend the person you are talking about is listening. That will totally change what you say. Then you will be living the life of Proverbs 16:24: "Pleasant words are a honeycomb, sweet to the soul and healing to the bones."

11:22 PM - 15 comments - 9 Kudos - Add Comment

Subject: RE: #26 How do I stay friends with my ex without making my new bf/gf jealous?
Date: Tuesday, November 7, 2006 2:58 AM
From: Live conference
To: 'Justin Lookadoo' <emily@Lookadoo.com>
Conversation: Prom Dates

[handwritten: there are Always People who argue with THIS? Naïve? Stupid? Dangerous?]

You can't. If you break up with someone and go straight into dating someone else, the ex will always be on the new one's mind. You kinda have to give it some time. Get a little distance between you and your ex before you start trying to build a friendship. This will help close the deal for you, and it will help your new crush relax.

[handwritten: Definitely]

Plus, it's all about respect. Do you really respect your new crush? If so, you don't want to put them in a position where they have to question what's going on or feel uncomfortable.

For me, I never stayed really close friends with my exes. I may talk with them, but you wouldn't call us good friends. That's because I knew I liked something about that person or I wouldn't have gone out with them. And I was smart enough to know that even though we broke up, in the right situation at the right moment something could spark again. I didn't want to put myself in a position to be tempted, and I definitely didn't want to put my new gf (and now my wife) in a position to have to worry.

[handwritten, vertical: they will put themselves in situations to someone it will be a big deal!]

jlook

Justin Lookadoo
Buy Justin's hit new release **97**

Things To Do:

☐
☐ What is your view on
☐ Christians dating
☐ non-Christians?
☐
☐
☐
☐
☐

I just stick with the Bible on this one.

Let me give you a little setup. If you are a follower of Christ, then you are righteous. That means that Jesus has made you right to God. Anyone who has not made Jesus the director of their life is directed by wickedness. "He who is not with me is against me," Jesus said (Matthew 12:30). There is no middle ground. It's righteousness or wickedness. Light or dark. Anyone who has given control of their life to Jesus is in the light. If not, it's dark. No gray.

So when you ask about Christians dating non-Christians, I have to go to 2 Corinthians 6:14: "Do not be yoked together with unbelievers. For what do righteousness and wickedness have in common? Or what fellowship can light have with darkness?"

That's pretty clear. And I love the way Eugene Peterson breaks it down in *The Message*: "Don't become partners with those who reject God. How can you make a partnership out of right and wrong? That's not partnership; that's war. Is light best friends with dark?"

I know sometimes it seems like the other person is better when you are in their life. They stop drinking, they go to church, they try to be better, so you think this is your heavenly cue that you are supposed to be together. For those confusing situations, check out 1 Corinthians 15:33: "Do not be misled: 'Bad company corrupts good character.'" They will bring you down more than you could ever bring them up, and if you break up, they will probably go back to their old ways. That is not a sign that you are supposed to stay with the person to make them better. It's a sign that they are faking a change to be with you. This is not saying the person you're wondering about is a horrible person. But spiritually, they are not going the same direction as you.

Here's the scenario. What if you go out with this person who is not a follower of Christ, and you start really liking each other, and you end up married? What if nothing ever changes? You are stuck in a covenant with someone who sees the world a totally different way. Remember how Eugene Peterson said it—"That's not partnership; that's war." You will never have total connection and intimacy, and they are not moving toward the same eternal destination as you are.

Thought: a lot of people think that if they get really close to a person, then they will see Jesus and will give their lives over to him. But I think this is more like the truth: if you are going out with someone for a while and you get really close and are totally into each other, the thought is more like, *You like me just the way I am without being a Christian, so why change?*

Another thought: if you are going out with a nonbeliever and you don't drift apart, you might want to question your growth and commitment as a follower of Christ. Just a thought.

Is Kissing Considered cheating?

You have got to be joking! Please tell me you are not serious.
Think about this: would you kiss someone in front of your bf
or gf? Even better, imagine it's your wedding day, the minister
dude says, "You may kiss the bride," and the groom grabs a
girl in the audience and starts kissing her. Is kissing considered
cheating? Go away.

Did you know Emily
owned a snake
until it got too big.
It was 11½ feet long
and almost 100 pounds.

Subject: RE: #29 Why does my girlfriend get mad when I talk to other girls?

Date: Monday, October 2, 2006 8:30 PM

From: Live conference

To: 'Justin Lookadoo' <emily@Lookadoo.com>

Conversation: Prom Dates

Why do you get mad when your girlfriend talks to other guys? Duh!

You and your crush are relatively new at this whole relationship thing, and you are both trying to figure out what this thing is all about. The last thing you want to see is the person you're crushing on chatting it up with the competition.

jlook

Justin Lookadoo
Check out Justin's bestselling book *Dateable: are you? are they?*

So much for Common Sense.

Lookadoo

Last Updated:
July 31, 2007

Send Message
Instant Message
Email to a Friend
Subscribe
Invite to My Blog

Gender: Male
Status: Married
Age: 101
Sign: Pisces

City: McKinney
State: TEXAS
Country: US

Signup Date:
02/17/06

Wednesday, June 20, 2007

#30 If me and my gf want to have a godly relationship, how do we do it? Could you give me some real ideas?

Okay, let me say this: there is no such thing as a godly relationship. Relationships cannot be godly. People can, but relationships can't. Relationships can bring glory to God or they can disgrace him, but there's no such thing as a godly relationship. Now, there can be two godly people who are in a relationship. And when that happens, God is being honored, and we call that a godly relationship. But it really isn't about the relationship; it's about the people in the relationship.

Here is where most people mess up: You have a person who is looking for answers. They have a void they are trying to fill. They are trying to feel beautiful and desired, or they are trying to confirm that they are a real man in today's world. They are trying to find comfort, closeness, or companionship. They have a hole they need filled. They hook up with another person who is also struggling to find who they are and what their purpose is in this life. Now you have two people looking to fill the emptiness, and they come together and want a godly relationship. It can't happen that way.

Here, do this—or rather *don't* do this. You and your crush, don't pray together. Don't do a Bible study together. Don't memorize Scripture together. Now, wipe that confused look off your face and keep reading.

You want a godly relationship, right? Okay. How much time do you spend a day praying? Not you the couple but you the *you*. How do you pray? Do you just talk *at* God and tell him thank you for this and help me with that, or have you learned to shut up and listen? What is the last thing you heard God say to you? What are you studying in the Bible? I didn't ask what you are just blowing by just to say you read something. I mean, are you sitting down with a pen and paper and really digging into what the stuff means? Are you in church? Are you active, or do you go and zone out just so you can check the "I went to church" box?

What about your crush? How would they answer? No, not what have you done together—what are they doing on their own?

Until this starts happening individually, you will not have a godly relationship like you are wanting. Each person has to be doing their own thing.

Once you have that going, then make sure you do not have intimate prayer times and Bible studies together. Hey, where does intimate prayer time and Bible study happen? Yep, in quiet, secluded, intimate places. And going way deep spiritually creates a false sense of closeness that could lead you into some very tempting situations.

Okay, watch how all of this stuff comes together and see how a relationship that brings glory to God works. It's like this. The dude is doing his thing and connecting with God. At the same time, the girl is getting her voids filled by her heavenly Father. When they come together in a relationship, they will glorify God just by being who they are. They will go to see a movie and they'll ditch going to the top flick because they know the stars will sleep together and they don't want that stuff in their heads. They will go down to the homeless shelter and serve food because they know there is a need. When they get a frantic call about an emergency, they will stop and pray about it right there in the mall. Not alone in the car with the music going.

When they get home and her parents aren't there, they will either stay out in the front yard hanging out or he will go home until later. They won't put themselves in a position to fail physically. They will encourage each other, and they will defend others against rumors and negativity. If they break up, they will say nothing but good stuff about the other person.

Are you getting the visual here? Do you see this "godly relationship" at work? This brings honor to God, and it has nothing to do with the relationship.

Do everything in your power to become like Christ. And wait until you find someone else who is doing the same. Not just someone who is a Christian. Being a Christian is a great start, but the two of you have to be growing, praying, studying, and moving closer to being Christlike; then you will be able to have a relationship that brings glory to God. Otherwise you will be like a lot of discouraged people—two Christians hoping a relationship will make them stronger in their faith. It won't happen.

8:05 AM - 7 comments - 3 Kudos - Add Comment

If it won't last, then why bother?

You don't have to. In fact, it would probably be best if you didn't jump headfirst into the relational river until you are at a stage in your life where a solid relationship could be an option. But if you choose to date, it's not a bad thing. You get to learn a lot about yourself, about others, about life, and about how to interact. You get to see how you handle and like new situations. And hey, dating can be way fun if you don't take it so seriously.

Here is Justin and Emily at their #2 vacation spot, Mismaloya, outside of Puerta Vallarta.

Subject: RE: #32 When are you old enough to be in a serious relationship that could last?
Date: Saturday, May 20, 2006 4:45 PM
From: Live conference
To: 'Justin Lookadoo' <emily@Lookadoo.com>
Conversation: Prom Dates

Everyone wants to know when it is okay to date seriously. It's not an age; it's a stage. Here's the deal: if you are still living in your mama's house, eating your mama's food, and talking on your mama's phone, then you are not ready for a serious relationship. See, serious dating is like the minor leagues to marriage. And if you are not in a position to get married, you are playing in the wrong league. That's like a little kid playing T-ball thinking he's ready for the major leagues. He's not even in the game yet. So if you are not in that position, then you are not ready for a serious relationship.

And the reason I say it's a stage and not an age is because there are 35-year-old men still living in their mama's house, eating their mama's food, and talking on their mama's phone. They are not ready for a serious relationship.

jlook

Justin Lookadoo
Buy Justin's hit new release **97**

Subject: RE: #33 When a guy and a girl end their relationship, why do they say only mean things about each other?
Date: Thursday, November 23, 2006 6:36 PM
From: Live conference
To: 'Justin Lookadoo' <emily@Lookadoo.com>
Conversation: Prom Dates

This is how people try to protect their pride and hide their hurt. It doesn't work like we think it does. And usually it starts when someone tells one of the people who just broke up what they heard the other person say about them, and then that person spouts off about all the stuff they hate about the other person. Okay, but if the person was that horrible, you wouldn't have gone out with them in the first place.

Here's the deal: you can tell a lot more about what a person is like when they break up with someone than you can while they are in a relationship. If you watch someone destroy their ex, do not go out with that person. They will end up destroying you.

And if you are the one breaking up, hold on to your pride and honor, especially as a follower of Christ, and do what your mama told you when you were a kid: "If you can't say anything nice, don't say anything at all."

jlook

Justin Lookadoo
**Order your copy of the
3-part Dateable DVD now!** product@lookadoo.com

look up VERSE About Pride comes Before the fall.

Thursday, December 14, 2006

#34 What do you think about starting a relationship before going to college, like if one is leaving and the other one is staying?

Not smart. That's like saying you are going to start paying for this car, but you are not going to take it, you are going to leave it behind.

Here's the deal. Whenever someone is going to college and they have a bf/gf somewhere else, my question is always, "Do you want to experience college life fully, or do you want to miss out?" If you answer that question, you will know what you should do.

If you say you want to have a full college experience, you can't really do that if you are always focused on, worried about, and involved with someone who is somewhere else. Your life will seem like it is anchored down, and you won't be able to freely move like you want.

9:42 PM - 5 comments - 13 Kudos - Add Comment

Is it okay to call from the driveway to have my girlfriend meet me outside?

Only if you want to prove what a lame loser you are. What are you, lazy or scared? You must be one of them, and both are signs that you don't have what it takes to go out with a girl. Go to the door, and talk with her parents. Even if she runs out and says, "Let's go," tell her, "I just want to say hi to your parents." Be a man.

Girls, if your dude just hits you on the cell or texts you to come out, he is a wuss, and you need to stop going out with him until he thinks enough of you not to treat you like a cheeseburger at a nasty fast food joint.

Subject: RE: #36 What is courting and what are its benefits? Please explain the details of how it's done.
Date: Wednesday, February 14, 2007 11:11 PM
From: Live conference
To: 'Justin Lookadoo' <emily@Lookadoo.com>
Conversation: Prom Dates

Uh . . . I have no idea. You ask a bunch of people who say they don't date but they court, and you are going to get a bunch of different answers. And most of the answers that I have heard make it sound like courting is really just boring dating.

jlook

Justin Lookadoo
Check out Justin's bestselling book **Dateable: are you? are they?**

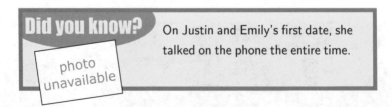

Did you know? On Justin and Emily's first date, she talked on the phone the entire time.

photo unavailable

Sunday, January 21, 2007

#37 I want to break up with my girlfriend, but I don't want to hurt her feelings. I tried to just stop talking to her, but it didn't work. What can I do?

Okay, you didn't stop talking to her because you didn't want to hurt her. You did that because you didn't have the *who-ha's* to tell her you wanted to break up. Dude, get a little manhood and stop being a pansy. You have to tell her that the relationship is over. Don't just stop talking to her, you dork. Tell her. No, don't go empty-handed. Go get *The Dirt on Breaking Up*. It will help you tremendously on knowing how to do it and do it smoothly without dragging it out or destroying each other.

5:15 PM - **9 comments** - **10 Kudos** - **Add Comment**

Monday, January 22, 2007

Here is a cover of the Breaking Up book.

9:35 PM - **4 comments** - **2087 Kudos** - **Add Comment**

Subject: RE: #38 How do you still maintain a normal friendship with a guy after you break up?
Date: Monday, March 26, 2007 10:40 PM
From: Live conference
To: 'Justin Lookadoo' <emily@Lookadoo.com>
Conversation: Prom Dates

You don't. Sorry, but you can't just go backwards and expect everything to be like it was.

And check this out: the intensity of the relationship has to equal the intensity of the separation. If you went out with someone twice, you don't have to have much separation. But if you really poured a lot into this relationship, then the separation has to be intense and complete.

Maybe later you will be able to have some sort of relationship with the person, but it won't be like it was. Sorry.

jlook

Justin Lookadoo
See what is happening at www.Lookadoo.com

Is it weird not to date?

Not at all. Actually, it's perfect. Most people think they have to date. They are searching for who they are, trying to find out what their life is all about. Then they jump into dating someone who is doing the same thing. I think most of the time this actually delays them in understanding who they are.

If you choose not to date, then you actually get to focus on you. You get to know yourself without someone else cluttering up your vision. So not dating is actually the best answer.

Did you know Emily glued her eyes shut with hot candle wax.

Lookadoo

Last Updated:
July 31, 2007

Send Message
Instant Message
Email to a Friend
Subscribe
Invite to My Blog

Gender: Male
Status: Married
Age: 101
Sign: Pisces

City: McKinney
State: TEXAS
Country: US

Signup Date:
02/17/06

Monday, April 23, 2007

#40 If you think that not dating is better than dating, then why do you spend so much time telling people how to date?

Yes, for the most part not dating is the right answer. But I know that very few people can pull that off. So my job is to tell young people how to date without pouring too much into it and hurting themselves in the process.

11:37 AM - 8 comments - 3 Kudos - Add Comment

Tuesday, April 24, 2007

Want to know the real deal?

Get *Dateable: are you? are they?* It will open your eyes.

5:30 PM - 18 comments - 1,754 Kudos - Add Comment

Sunday, May 20, 2007

#41 Most of this stuff you say about dating is focused on high school relationships. Do these rules ever change?

Yes, the rules do change. At some point it will be able to last. And when that happens, then you have to put a lot into the marriage. You don't shut people out to protect your heart. The depth you can love will be in relation to the depth you are willing to hurt.

But a lot of stuff never changes. Girls still build fantasy worlds. Guys still tell girls what they think she wants to hear. Girls are always crazy and guys are always jerks—it's just that we learn to control it better. The sex stuff never changes. Just because you are older or even have gone through a divorce, God doesn't change the rules for you when it comes to the sex issues.

So yes, some things change—and some things never change.

4:20 PM - 14 comments - 2 Kudos - Add Comment

**Subject: RE: #42 What's the big deal about marriage?
I mean, isn't it just a word and a document?**
Date: Sunday, July 1, 2007 1:23 AM
From: Live conference
To: 'Justin Lookadoo' <emily@Lookadoo.com>
Conversation: Prom Dates

Come on, that's like saying, "What's the big deal about being the president? Isn't it just a word and a document? I mean, you just put your hand on a Bible, say some words, sign a piece of paper, and you're done." Well, if that is true, I need you to get your assistant to get on the phone and have your plane, *Air Force One*, pick you up and take you to meet with the prime minister of Great Britain. Yeah, it ain't happening. Why? Because being president is a lot more than just words and a document. It is an oath. To get that clear, you have to know what an oath is. Check out the definition of *oath* I grabbed from Merriam-Webster Online:

> oath: a solemn usually formal calling upon God or a god to witness to the truth of what one says or to witness that one sincerely intends to do what one says

Look at that again. An oath is a call upon God to witness that you sincerely intend to do what you say. It's not just a word and a document. It's calling on God to witness your promise and dedication.

Marriage is the same thing. You are taking an oath. And even more than that, you are making a covenant with God. Now in the Bible a covenant was the most binding, intimate contract with God. When two people

Get stuffed Animal to pull APART & PLACE IN 2 Rows

entered into a covenant, they would sacrifice an animal and place the parts in two rows, and then they would walk down the middle. This represented "the walk of death." It meant that the two would enter into this commitment until death. And if either one were to break the covenant, then God would take their life as they did the animal. It was a pretty heavy deal.

The problem is that we don't take deals with God very seriously. Back in the day you could see the serious consequences. But God shows us grace and compassion. And we think that grace means he really doesn't care what we do, so we can make a covenant like marriage and then when we want out, hey, God doesn't really mind. He understands. So we just blow God off and think that he doesn't notice, doesn't care, or is just weak. He does notice. He does care. And trust me, he's not weak.

Let's go back to the president thing. When you really take the oath and make the covenant, then you get a lot of privileges and responsibilities that come with the commitment. It's the same way with marriage. Once you make that covenant with the other person and before God, then you get the privileges and responsibilities that come with it. Like sex. Like commitment. Like loving the person forever—not just the feeling of love but every aspect of love that is described in 1 Corinthians 13:4-7: "Love is patient, love is kind. It does not envy, it does not boast, it is not proud. It is not rude, it is not self-seeking, it is not easily angered, it keeps no record of wrongs. Love does not delight in evil but rejoices with the truth. It always protects, always trusts, always hopes, always perseveres." That's what love is. That's what happens in a marriage—not a throwaway marriage but a real one.

Marriage is a word and a document. But it is way more. It is a covenant with God that cannot be broken without a death. It may not be our physical death anymore because of God's grace, but there is a death—his Son's. Don't take it lightly.

jlook

Justin Lookadoo
Check out Justin's bestselling book *Dateable: are you? are they?*

Do a skit where we DRESS UP in tux & WEDDING DRESS & WALK BETWEEN DEAD ANIMALS.

Did you know? Emily went to the hospital more times in her first year of marriage than Justin has in his entire life.

The Horizontal Tango
[sex and all that]

Did you KNOW?

Emily's dad
is an
internationally
known sculptor.
Check out his art
at www.herbgoldman.com

Subject: RE: #43 Why do girls feel that the only way to be popular is to do nasty stuff with guys?
Date: Tuesday, October 10, 2006 5:47 PM
From: Live conference
To: 'Justin Lookadoo' <emily@Lookadoo.com>
Conversation: The Horizontal Tango

They don't. A girl who acts this way is totally misin-terpreting affection as love. And any time a guy asks her to share something intimate and secret with him, she perceives that as a deep connection and trust, and she feels the guy really likes her.

But girls know that doing this stuff isn't a sling-shot to popularity because among girls, this isn't a badge of honor. In the girl circle they want to be seen as pure, popular, desired, and strong. They do not sit around and talk about how easy, slutty, and insecure they are and how they will do anything with a guy that makes them feel accepted and loved. So it's really not about popularity. It's about af-fection and love.

Now, let me throw out a couple of disclaimers. Sure, a few girls believe that guys like them more when they use their body. Guys, where do you think they got that idea? It wasn't from other girls. Yeah, it was from guys. Guys are the ones destroying girls like this. So listen fellas, it's time to stand up and be men and protect girls instead of using them. We are supposed to protect and honor girls so when the time comes for a girl to be married, she is able to give herself to her husband and "present her to himself as a radiant church, without stain or wrinkle or any other blemish, but holy and blameless" (Ephesians

REFER HER TO "THE NAKED TRUTH" DVD

5:27). Fellas, you don't want to be the one that God sees when she gives herself and she has some blemishes, dirt, and scars on her. Oh, you *don't* want God to hold you responsible—but guys, he will.

jlook

Justin Lookadoo
Order your copy of the
3-part Dateable DVD now! *product@lookadoo.com*

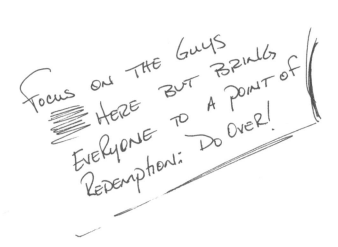

FOCUS ON THE GUYS HERE BUT BRING EVERYONE TO A POINT OF REDEMPTION: DO OVER!

Did you know? While skydiving, Emily almost landed in a prison.

Lookadoo

Last Updated:
July 31, 2007

Send Message
Instant Message
Email to a Friend
Subscribe
Invite to My Blog

Gender: Male
Status: Married
Age: 101
Sign: Pisces

City: McKinney
State: TEXAS
Country: US

Signup Date:
02/17/06

Monday, November 6, 2006

#44 What if I want to stop doing physical things or stop having sex with my bf/gf? Can we just start over and be okay?

I have asked tons and tons of people this question. And their answers were:

Yes. There is no reason you can't confess, forgive, and start over.

or

No. Absolutely not. It's impossible.

Everyone in the "Yes" group were people who had never experienced this before. And that is a great thing. They had never gone too far, and they were totally wrapped up in God's ability to do anything, to repair anything, and they believed that the relationship can go on.

Everyone in the "No" group were people who had been there. They had gone too far. They got into the physical side of a relationship and then decided to backtrack. They believe in God's ability to do anything as well, but their issue is not God's ability but their own flesh and desires. They all said that you will stop a little while out of guilt or shame, and you will make promises and commitments to purity, and you will be totally serious in the moment. But it won't take long to slide into the same physical relationship as before.

Like an old gentleman I know once told me, "Boy, if you go to the barbershop long enough, eventually you'll get a haircut." Think about it. It will make sense.

So here's what I think. Stay in the "Yes" group. Don't put yourself in a situation where you'll have to test your theory.

Because the people in the "No" group got there through pain and hurt.

One final thing. What we are talking about is a relationship that causes us to be tempted and to fall. Matthew 5:29 says, "If your right eye causes you to sin, gouge it out and throw it away. It is better for you to lose one part of your body than for your whole body to be thrown into hell." If that is God's take on a part of our body that causes us to sin, what do you think his view will be of a crush that causes us to sin?

8:52 PM - **8 comments** - **12 Kudos** - **Add Comment**

How can I say no when someone asks me to have sex?

Uh . . . "NO."

"No way."

Look confused and disgusted and say, "With you?"

"Love to. When are we getting married?"

"Let me call my dad and ask him if it's all right."

"I'm sure you asked Jesus about it. What did he tell you?"

"Do you mind if I pray during it?"

Act as if you are about to spew, put your hand over your mouth, and say, "I just ate."

"What do you want to name the baby?"

Laugh uncontrollably. When they ask, "What's wrong?" say, "I'm sorry, I was just picturing you naked."

Subject: RE: #46 Why do adults make sex sound so horrible?
Date: Monday, June 18, 2007 9:08 AM
From: Live conference
To: 'Justin Lookadoo' <emily@Lookadoo.com>
Conversation: The Horizontal Tango

Mom will be proud to read that.

My opinion is that a lot of adults haven't had great sex, and if they have, they don't know what to say about it. So let me be the one to tell you that even bad sex is good sex. But that is exclusively inside the boundaries of marriage. If you are married, GAME ON! Do as much or as little as you want. You can go freaky, you can go romantic, you can go wherever you want to go.

Just go.

Sex is fun. It brings two people together. You can laugh, you can grow, and you can even be in the middle of sex and break out into prayer or singing praise. I know it's weird to think about. But the reason it's weird is because you're not married. This stuff can't happen when you are in the middle of sin. But when you're in the middle of God's anointing called marriage, it can definitely happen.

Listen, if you start doing anything before you are married, it will start driving a wedge between the two of you. It may happen immediately, like he has sex with you and dumps you, or it may take a while. But it will happen.

And let's really be honest. If you have sex, there will always be a point of comparison. A lot of times people say their sex life goes downhill after they get married. If it does, usually that's because they are comparing it to every other time and person. Hey, if you love cheesecake and you have tried a whole bunch of them and then you are stuck with one cheesecake that you will have for the rest of your life, then you will compare it with the other cheesecakes you've had. It will happen automatically.

Flip it. If you've never had cheesecake and the first one you had was the one you were going to have your entire life, it would blow your mind. It wouldn't matter if it were the second best or the fourth worst, you would swear it was the best cheesecake ever made, and you wouldn't care what anyone else said. Same with sex.

When you do it in the safety and commitment of a secure marriage, then sex will be one of the most incredible experiences you'll have. Remember, God created sex and he said, "It is good," and Adam and Eve shouted, "Yes it is!"

jlook

Justin Lookadoo
See what is happening at www.Lookadoo.com

ADD STUFF ABOUT YOU DON'T COMPARE ALL THINGS ALL THE TIME!

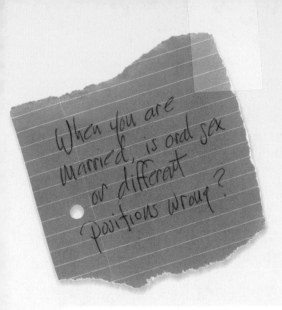

When you are married, is oral sex or different positions wrong?

Hey, when you are married, game on! Go for it. Be as crazy as you want to be. But you are definitely right: it's a married game.

Did you know one of Justin and Emily's favorite games is Catch Phrase.

Subject: RE: #48 What do women really wear on their wedding nights?

Date: Wednesday, July 4, 2007 12:07 AM

From: Live conference

To: 'Justin Lookadoo' <emily@Lookadoo.com>

Conversation: The Horizontal Tango

Girls, hear me now and believe me later. *It doesn't matter!*

We appreciate the effort and the beauty. We love the sexy stuff. But listen, this guy says he loves you and wants to spend the rest of his life with you. To him you are going to be perfect.

On our wedding night Emily wore red-and-white striped flannel pajamas. She looked like one of Santa's elves. And she was the most beautiful girl I had ever seen. So ladies, don't worry.

jlook

Justin Lookadoo
Buy Justin's hit new release **97**

Wednesday, May 23, 2007

#49 If a girl wants to get physical with me, what should I do?

Throw your hands in the air and run around in a circle yelling, "Stranger! Danger! Stranger! Danger!"

Now, this may not help grow this relationship, but it will make her stop. And that's pretty much the picture we get from 1 Corinthians 6:18: "Flee from sexual immorality." It doesn't say fight it, ignore it, repress it, or pray about it. It says *RUN*!

If that's not your favorite option, let me go a little further. You are going to run into more and more sexually aggressive girls. And as a guy, it will be tough to walk away from it. So here's my question. Are you a man? Do you have what it takes to stand up and make the tough calls?

Any hunters out there? Yeah, the one guy reading this book sitting in a camouflage outfit, face painted and branches duct taped to his hat, I'm talking to you. For the rest of you, this will still make sense.

If you're a big deer hunter, imagine if a deer walks into your house, opens the freezer, squeezes himself in, whistles at you, and shouts, "Hey, come in here and shoot me!" Most guys would be like, "Uh . . . okay." Not because it was fun, exciting, fulfilling, or even a challenge but simply because it was easy.

That's the same way it is when a girl throws herself at you. A lot of guys will go with it not because they like the girl or she is something special that he desires but simply because she's easy.

Guys, if you are serious about wanting to know what you can do, try talking to her. I know that's a little weird, but girls like to talk. So why not try it?

The next big question—"What do I say?" (Wow, I'm a mind reader.)

Tell her that her doing physical things with you won't make you like her more. And fill her in on our guy secret that if she gets into physical stuff with guys, most of them will take it, not because they like her but because it's easy. Then throw in something like this: "But you know, I'm not like other guys. I'm a bigger man than that. And if I'm going to like you, I want to like you because I know you, not because I like the sexual stuff you do." This will put you in a whole different world in her eyes.

Warning: If you say this, it may make her like you even more. And remember that she thinks physical things must happen if you like her. Stay strong. This is not all about her. It's about you being a man who is powerful and who honors her as God's princess.

Girls, if you are way too pushy in your physical relationship or in the way you dress, let me explain a couple of guy options that might be going on.

* He could be a good guy who wants to honor you and God, and he will start pushing you away. The more you push him, the more he will try to push back so he can stay strong. The same for your actions and the way you dress. The really good dude could start pushing you away because he knows he can't handle the flesh factory that you are showing him. Guys, if you get in this sitch, let her know that her dress and actions are killing you and your relationship.

* He will take it full on, and he will get bored with you quick. Guys, this is where you have the chance to show that you are bold, that you have what it takes to be a man and fight in God's war. Tell her that if you do jump in, you will like it for a minute, but soon you will get bored and the relationship will be over. You're a guy. That's what happens. Try being honest and see what happens.

<u>3:20 PM</u> - <u>3 comments</u> - <u>3 Kudos</u> - <u>Add Comment</u>

Subject: RE: #50 When is the right time to have sex?
Date: Thursday, March 29, 2007 3:17 PM
From: Live conference
To: 'Justin Lookadoo' <emily@Lookadoo.com>
Conversation: The Horizontal Tango

When you are in love. Oh, sorry, that's not it.

It's when you are ready . . . aw, that's crap too.

The only time you are ready to have sex is when you are married. That means rings, a wedding, a deal between you and God that this is forever. That's when it is okay to have sex. Any other time there will be guilt, shame, confusion, and uncertainty, and you will be in a fog that will cloud what you feel about the relationship.

jlook

Justin Lookadoo
Check out Justin's bestselling book *Dateable: are you? are they?*

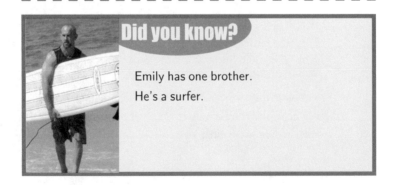

Did you know?

Emily has one brother.
He's a surfer.

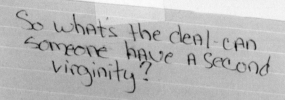

So what's the deal—can someone have a second virginity?

Yes and no. We have to look at what virginity really is. We usually only focus on the physical, but that's only part of the story. We have to look at the triad of physical, emotional, and spiritual. And here are the basics.

Physical—this is all on you

Spiritual—this is God's deal

Emotional—this is where God's deal connects to your world

Let's break it down.

PHYSICAL. The intense focus on physical virginity has helped feed the lust lie that we can do everything else in the world and we can do it in every way possible as long as a penis does not get inserted into a vagina. If we keep it like that we are still virgins. No, we're not!

I think we put way too much focus on the physical virginity. I know we have to focus on the physical because we live in the physical world, but I think this is the weakest of the three parts of virginity.

With that little rant thrown out there, I have to say that physically, you will not get a do-over with your virginity. This is just a guess here, but I would imagine that God isn't going to come down and turn back time on the physical stuff. We all pretty much understand the dynamics here. You have sex, you are no longer a virgin. You'll never be a physical virgin again. I am talking about everything here from groping and fondling to oral sex, anal sex, or just regular sex. You cannot go back, and you have to deal with the physical consequences. That could mean HIV, herpes, pregnancy, or just knowing that you have given away something precious. That also means having to deal with the rumors and embarrassment when people talk about what you did. God will not swoop down and wipe out everyone's knowledge of it so you can start over. These are all physical consequences.

I know that is a downer, but there is hope.

SPIRITUAL. Can you be a virgin again spiritually? Not really. Oh, don't get all upset just yet. That's not a bad thing; it's a God thing. A second spiritual virginity is not really a second anything. It's a total spiritual newness. And the spiritual side is the most crucial part of the virginity triad.

If you do push any of the physical limits, it disconnects you from God. It is sin, and that's what sin does. Our physical actions have spiritual consequences. This isn't just isolated to throwing clothes outside of marriage. That's the way it is with any sin.

A lot of people who are playing in the sin pool say they don't feel shut off from God. Sometimes that's because they don't notice they are disconnected. They pray, sing praise songs, read the Bible, and then have oral sex with their girlfriend and claim to be connected to God. Well, this phony world they have built has become their comfort zone. Romans 6:23 says, "For the wages of sin is death, but the gift of God is

eternal life in Christ Jesus our Lord." One of the first things to die is that connection with God.

The question here is about a second virginity. I told you that spiritually it wouldn't happen that way. Watch this: "If we confess our sins, he is faithful and just and will forgive us our sins and purify us from all unrighteousness" (1 John 1:9). That doesn't mean you are just scrubbed. That means it's done, you have a complete newness. Get this. "As far as the east is from the west, so far has he removed our transgressions from us" (Psalm 103:12). Do you get that? Once you confess, it's gone.

Check it. You spill your half-frap, double-foam, hi-lo, upside-down lattecappuccino all over the front of your white shirt. You rush it to the cleaners and say, "Please get this out. I love this shirt." You come back and there is still a noticeable stain on the front. It's not as horrific as it was, but you can still see evidence of the mishap. That is *not* the way God cleanses you spiritually. Once you repent and get God's forgiveness, in the spiritual world there is no evidence that your sin was there. It is as far away as the east is from the west. It's gone.

Imagine if you take that jacked-up shirt to the cleaners, and when you come back to get your shirt, you lift it up and there is a huge hole cut out of it. You do a little freak-out dance and ask him what happened. He smiles and tells you he got the stain out. All he had to do was cut out the stained part and he was done. That is not the kind of cleansing God does either. He doesn't just cut that part out of you and leave you with this spiritual void where you feel empty.

Here's what God does. You take the shirt in, you come back, and he hands you an amazing shirt. There are no stains. No blemishes. No history that shows what might have happened. In fact, you think he might have handed you a brand-new shirt. The more you look at it, the more sure you become that this isn't just a cleaned-up old shirt. This is your shirt, only brand-new. That's the way God forgives. Completely. With no record.

Spiritually, you are totally healed. Your spiritual virginity is restored. In fact, in the God realm you are totally and completely whole. That is a cool thing about God.

EMOTIONAL. Emotionally, it's a little different story. The spiritual part is heavy on the God side. We repent and he does everything else. The physical, we control by our actions, so it is heavy on our side. The emotional part is heavy on both sides.

The emotional scars of your sin can last a lifetime. We can be healed, but it is going to take work on our part and God's. Every choice you make and everything you do or that is done to you makes impressions on your mentals and emotions. Good and bad. When you give your body away or do things that are sexual before you are married, it creates a wound. Just like getting cut with a knife. And you know, when you first get sliced open, it hurts. Some pain goes along with it. But you can doctor it up, bandage it, protect it, and with time it will heal. Yes, you will have a scar. But scars tend to fade with time. They seem to be less and less noticeable until you pretty much forget about them. You will eventually have to hunt to find where the scar was.

That is the same way sex works with your emotions. And it doesn't have to be going all the way. It can be just feeling around on each other. Doing physical stuff cuts you emotionally. In the beginning you will have pain. It will come with guilt, humiliation, shame, anger, a desire to never do it again along with a desire to do it, confusion—and you really can't handle it all. These are open wounds that you will have to deal with. You will have to ask God for forgiveness, but even tougher, you will have to forgive yourself. You will have to protect yourself from going back to the sin and cutting yourself again.

Your emotions can't handle being disconnected from God. And they can't handle the fact that they are getting ripped apart. So what happens is that they snap into survival mode, and you have to do something quick. You have to immediately stop what you are doing and totally get away from it. This will make you deal with the guilt and shame, and you will feel horrible because you have compromised yourself. This will be a tough thing to do, and it's scary.

Or you might try to push down all of those emotions, shove down the feelings, and quickly convince yourself that you are in control. And to make yourself feel powerful you have to repeat doing it over and over until you get calloused and desensitized. Every time you do something else and guilt creeps in, you have to cover it up with lies. Like, "She really enjoys doing that with me." "We love each other." "He likes me just the way I am." And the ever-popular lie, "I'm glad that we aren't having sex." All of this because your emotional virginity has been destroyed. Now you have to go into justification and rationalization modes of self-preservation.

Healing your emotional virginity will take time and effort. You have to accept the fact that you were wrong, embrace how horrible it feels, and repent and come to God for forgiveness. You have to forgive yourself, and you'll have to do that a thousand times. And remember, your *scars* are not your identity. Just because you messed up doesn't mean you're a screwup. That is not who you are. It will take some time. You will have to give this over to God and let him show you how wonderful you are. He can make you whole.

So back to the question you probably forgot by now. **Can you have a second virginity?** Physically, no; you live with the earthly consequences. Spiritually, definitely; God will do that immediately when you repent. Emotionally, yes, but it will take time for the scars to heal.

And there you have it.

Did you know Justin's mom is the superintendent of schools in Mineola, Texas.

Lookadoo

Last Updated:
July 31, 2007

Send Message
Instant Message
Email to a Friend
Subscribe
Invite to My Blog

Gender: Male
Status: Married
Age: 101
Sign: Pisces

City: McKinney
State: TEXAS
Country: US

Signup Date:
02/17/06

Friday, June 22, 2007

#52 If you should know everything about a person and what they're like and how they'll treat you, then why save sex for marriage if that bond can show you that you really may not be meant for each other?

You are right. Sex is a bond that is set up to help cement a relationship. To seal the deal. And I like your example of the bond, the glue, so let's go with that.

If you are not married, you are two separate objects, her and him. If you add in the bond of sex, it puts super glue on her and super glue on him. They are still two separate objects trying to figure out if they should be one. They still haven't come together. So what happens? The glue dries, leaving behind this hard, jagged surface. Say your relationship doesn't work out. The process happens again. Sex. Glue. It dries on each surface, but they are still separate. The relational surface of each person gets even more built up with dried gunk.

Finally you play it right and you get married. You have sex. The glue goes on her side and on his side, and they come together as one inside a marriage. The bond between the two isn't nearly as strong because of all the dried-up glue on each surface. It's not a smooth, clean surface attached to a smooth, clean surface. It's rough on rough, and the bond is not as strong as it was supposed to be. Does that mean the bond will rip apart? No, not always. But it does mean that it will take more work and relational maintenance to deal with the cracked past, insecurities, hurts, and gunk that is left from the past sexual decisions.

Maybe you are one of those people sitting there thinking, *That's the point. We have to see if the bond will hold.* Okay, fine, let's go your way. Sex creates a bond, and you need to know if that bond will be strong enough to keep you together. You have sex and the super glue goes on her and on him. The two people are glued together. Inevitably, you get tired of the person or something happens that causes you to break up. Think about it. Two people who were super glued together now have to be ripped apart. Hey, if you glue your hands together by accident, you will have some horrible ripping of flesh, major damage, maybe even a little trip to the hospital to try to get the two separated. Same way with you and sex. These two will be ripped apart with some major emotional and maybe even physical damage.

Sex is never a deal breaker once you get into marriage. Especially if you have done it God's way and saved it for marriage. When it happens, it will be two clean surfaces stuck together for eternity. And if you have already gone too far, don't just keep doing it. Stop adding more yuck to the surfaces. Step out of that and save yourself for God's best, his plan and his way to totally great sex.

11:17 AM - 14 comments - 4 Kudos - Add Comment

Yes. That's why it's called "oral sex." Not "oral knitting."

Oral sex is one of the biggest things in relationships that is destroying girls today. And guys, this is not the girls' problem. This is the guys' problem.

Girls are looking for the best way to get a guy to like them. And for some reason they have come to the conclusion that if they start doing physical stuff with a guy, then he will like them more. And fellas, where do you think girls came up with this idea? It wasn't from them sitting around with their girlfriends discussing it. No, it came from us. Guys, we have convinced girls that if they want to get a guy to like them, then they have to get physical.

It's time for me to let out a little guys' secret. Girls, understand this. If you start doing physical things with guys, believe me, we do not like you more. I know you think we do, but ladies, we don't. Well, hold on. Let me change that. If you start getting physical with guys we will like *being* with you more. But ladies, we don't give a rip about who *you* are. We like you because *you're easy*. Why would a dude want to have to go somewhere else and have to work when you're giving it away for free?

And girls, you need to know this. Whatever you are doing physically with your little boyfriend . . . all of his friends know. And they know in great detail. I know, ladies, it's different with you and your crush. He probably told you and you even believe that "This was something special between us." Yeah, and that is true, if by "us" you mean everyone reading this book. It is not "our little special secret." People know, and they're talking.

Think about this, girls. The question was about oral sex. If you are doing that with guys, you are no longer the sweet, beautiful girl with mystery and charm. You are the girl who will open her mouth for anyone. Just thought you should know.

Now, back to the real problem here. Guys, we are the problem. Guys, it's time you stood up and actually acted like a follower of Christ. You want to know what is really causing the destruction of girls? It's not oral sex. It's guys acting like they care about girls and then getting physical with them just to make their little egos feel better. Guys, stand up and be a man. That means making the tough call and saying no. That means you take the lead and stop asking stupid questions like "Is oral sex really sex?" You admit that what you're doing is wrong and you change it. Guys, this is the one area of relationships where you really have control.

And one parting thought, fellas. I wish every dad out there would stand up and take their role as a father seriously. Stop pansying around not wanting to upset your children. Hey, you're the father—act like it. Guys, I wish every father would do what one girl told me hers did, and I hope this goes through your mind every time you're with a girl. As the daughter ran out the door for her date, the dad shook the boy's hand, leaned in real close, and said, "Remember, whatever you do with her on your date, I'm gonna do to you when you get back. Go have fun."

For more on this stuff, check out The Dirt on Sex. The whole book is great, but oral sex stuff starts on page 36. You'll love it.

Thursday, April 19, 2007

#54 How far is too far?

The driveway. Next question.

Okay, the editor said I had to write more, so here goes.

Everyone reading this is smart enough to figure this out. But here's a little guide for you.

The next time you go out with your bf/gf, I want you to think about someone following you around with a little digi-cam taking photos of you guys. And after the date you go home and everyone is there—his family, her family, aunts, cousins, moms, dads, everyone. You sit down right beside your granny, they plug the camera into the TV, and you get to go through the slide show of your date.

Click.

"Look, Granny, there I am picking her up at the house. I opened the door for her."

Click.

"Look, Granny, there we are at the restaurant. I paid."

Click.

"Look, Granny, there we are at the movies. It was fun."

Click.

"Look, Granny, there we are driving home."

Click.

"Look, Granny, there we are kissing."

Click.

"Look, Granny, look right there. Yeah, see that? That's my tongue in her mouth."

Click.

"Look, Granny, that's my hand up her shirt."

Click.

"Look, Granny, there we are in the backseat. Yeah, that's her pants in the front."

Click.

"Look, Granny . . ."

At whatever point you get weird about telling your granny what happened, there's your line. And if you don't get weird about telling your granny anything, you need help.

So it's pretty basic. You can figure out pretty quick how far is too far.

1:20 AM - 6 comments - 3 Kudos - Add Comment

Did you know?

Emily spent her childhood summers at her grandparents' ranch in Lincoln, New Mexico (home of Billy the Kid), and Justin spent his summers on his grandparents' farm in Muleshoe, Texas.

I don't know, what is it said to be?

**Subject: RE: #56 Can a guy die from AIDS after using
"the pill"?**
Date: Saturday, October 28, 2006 12:27 PM
From: Live conference
To: 'Justin Lookadoo' <emily@Lookadoo.com>
Conversation: The Horizontal Tango

Yes. There is still no vaccine and no cure for
AIDS.

jlook

Justin Lookadoo
Order your copy of the
3-part Dateable DVD now! *product@lookadoo.com*

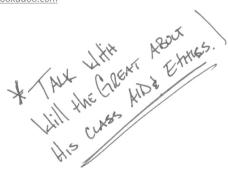

Tue, July 31, 2007 9:37 PM

Subject: RE: #57 Do oral sex and anal sex count against virginity?
Date: Monday, April 16, 2007 3:28 AM
From: Live conference
To: 'Justin Lookadoo' <emily@Lookadoo.com>
Conversation: The Horizontal Tango

Really?

Omigosh! I am guessing that you are a Christian and you are playing the we-can-do-anything-as-long-as-we-don't-have-sex game. In fact, I am sure that you are proud of yourself and your crush because you are not having sex—or at least you have convinced each other that you are not. Okay, stop playing games. Stop justifying everything you do by calling it by some other name. This is a perfect example of what is going on in Revelation 3:15-16 when God says: "I know your deeds, that you are neither cold nor hot. I wish you were either one or the other! So, because you are lukewarm—neither hot nor cold—I am about to spit you out of my mouth." Oh, and the word *spit*? That is the nice version. The original picture is vomit, puke, hurl, spew, blow chunks, barf.

Listen, if you are playing these little word games trying to convince yourself that you are pure, well, you are neither hot nor cold, you are lukewarm, and you make God want to puke. Hey, don't get mad at me. That's what God said, not me.

Now go check the other question about virginity. It will break it down for you.

jlook

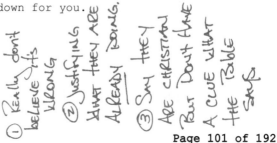

Why do so many Christians ask these kinds of questions.

1. Really don't believe it's wrong
2. Justifying what they are already doing.
3. Say they are Christian but don't have a clue what the Bible says

Monday, March 12, 2007

#58 Why do people make it seem like a big deal to have sex and get pregnant if we need the population to grow through the years?

First, we don't need the population to grow like we did back when God told Adam and Eve to be fruitful and multiply. Look around—we've done that pretty well. That was a beginning of the world issue, not so much a need today.

Second, sex isn't just for us to hump like rabbits and reproduce as fast as we can. A system was set up for having a child. A mother and a father are to teach, guide, and nurture the child. To show them an earthly vision of a holy God. That is to be done in the loving union of a man and woman. Not just a romp in the backseat and *oops! I'm pregnant*. Make sense?

10:04 PM - 5 comments - 4 Kudos - Add Comment

Do you think sex is
good a bad ?

I like it. But hey, I'm married.

Tue, July 31, 2007 9:38 PM

Subject: RE: #60 How do you know if the guy you like really likes you or if he is using you for sex?
Date: Friday, May 25, 2007 1:41 PM
From: Live conference
To: 'Justin Lookadoo' <emily@Lookadoo.com>
Conversation: The Horizontal Tango

You NEVER will.

Oh, I can't wait that long...

then Shutup! THAT'S what it takes!

If you are having sex with him, you don't know. In fact, if you are doing anything physical, you don't know if he likes you or if he just likes the goodies you're giving and is just holding on in hopes of getting more.

Here's your test: don't give the guy anything physically until you get married. When you do that, then what happens is that you get to know him and he gets to know you. That way if the relationship lasts, you will know that it's because you really like each other. If it ends, you will know that it was because the two of you really didn't work together. No guessing. No questions of whether sex clouded your vision.

jlook

Justin Lookadoo
Check out Justin's bestselling book *Dateable: are you? are they?*

Subject: RE: #61 Okay, if we can't have sex until marriage, can we do other stuff?

Date: Sunday, January 1, 2006 7:02 AM

From: Live conference

To: 'Justin Lookadoo' <emily@Lookadoo.com>

Conversation: The Horizontal Tango

Absolutely. You can talk, walk, go to the movies, shop, bike, hike, golf, play games, eat, make cards for your friends . . . there are thousands of things you can do.

jlook

Justin Lookadoo
Order your copy of the
3-part Dateable DVD now! *product@lookadoo.com*

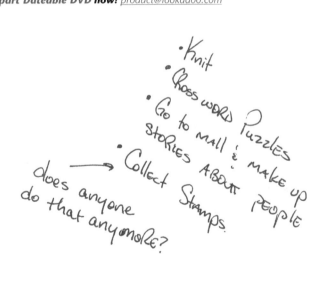

Friday, January 19, 2007

#62 If you had sex with somebody you thought you loved but in the end they cheated on you, is it okay to hate them?

No. If you hate someone, you are connected to them. Hate attaches a hook to that person so you are constantly attached to them. Forgiveness releases them. It says, "You don't owe me anything. I release you from any debt to me." That doesn't mean they get off scot-free; that means it is God's job to deal with them. Hey, your Father gets ticked when someone messes with his kid. So you let them go and forgive, and let God do whatever he does.

It is okay to be hurt, angry, upset, and a whole bunch of other emotions. That is natural. But let those emotions help motivate you and connect you to your Creator so that he can heal you.

Hopefully, you learned something very valuable through this. Love isn't a good reason to have sex. Neither is that fact that you are "ready," that you plan on getting married, or any other reason. The only time you are in the safety zone for sex is when you have committed to each other by getting married. The end.

3:17 PM - 7 comments - 16 Kudos - Add Comment

Superheroes
[a little x-ray vision
into the minds of the opposite sex]

Did you KNOW?

Emily was a ballerina when she was a little girl.

Did you KNOW?

Emily grew up to be a cheerleader.

Why do girls start so many rumors about other girls?

Oh, wow, there are a lot of reasons girls throw trash out there for others to pick up. Here are a few of the tops.

The Attention Invention: Believe it or not, the biggest reason may not be to destroy some other girl. Probably the top reason is so that the rumor starter can be the go-to girl and the center of attention. See, if you have a juicy story about someone and you are the source of the story, people will seek you out to find out what you know. A lot of girls get a charge out of that control and imaginary importance. Even if they have to invent the tales they share.

The Assassin: These people start rumors with one goal in mind—to hurt. They want to cause as much harm and pain as they can, so they will start a story that they know will rip someone's heart out. (Not many girls will actually admit to being this one, but trust me, there are a lot of them.)

The Crush Meter: This is the way some girls work. She starts the rumor that a guy likes her, and then she waits to see his reaction. If it is like, "No way," then she starts talking about how she would never like a dork like him.

If he is like, "Who told you that?" then she knows there must be some truth to it, so she starts trying to get closer to him.

The Manipulator: These are the girls who start rumors to try to break up a relationship or a crush. They spread dirt around hoping that the guy will wake up and see how lame the focus of his affection is so that maybe the Manipulator will have a chance. This may not come in the way of direct lies or rumors, but rather she takes every opportunity to make the other girl look less desirable. Oh, little comments like "She sure flirts with other guys a lot" and "I can't believe how slutty she dresses."

Girls, guys, everyone needs to understand that your words are powerful and you are responsible for what you say.

Proverbs 18:21: "The tongue has the power of life and death." You know this. You have seen people's hearts get crushed and their joy die because of what someone says. Maybe it was even you that died. That is a horrible thing to have happen to you, but that doesn't give you the right to do it also.

Proverbs 18:8: "The words of a gossip are like choice morsels; they go down to a man's inmost parts." This is why so many people tell stuff about other people. Satan has made it so that gossip tastes so sweet. But it is a direct violation of the Big Ten. Remember the Ten Commandments?

Exodus 20:16: "You shall not give false testimony against your neighbor." That means don't tell things that aren't true.

Proverbs 11:13: "A gossip betrays a confidence, but a trustworthy man keeps a secret." You want to know if one of your friends will keep your secrets, then look at what your friend tells you. Do they gossip? Do they spread other people's news? If so, they will tell your secrets. Hey, it's scriptural.

Proverbs 20:19: "A gossip betrays a confidence; so avoid a man who talks too much." No, that's not the same verse. The Bible is repeating itself to make sure you get it. And this verse tells you how to spot the gossip and who to stay away from—people who talk way too much. In fact, check this out.

Proverbs 10:19: "When words are many, sin is not absent, but he who holds his tongue is wise." If someone yakkity-yaks all the time, you can bet there is sin in the words. Again, I am just reading the Word here.

Proverbs 19:5: "A false witness will not go unpunished, and he who pours out lies will not go free." Don't be fooled. If you spread rumors, tell stories, or just "pass on information," you will not go unpunished. Your relationships will suffer. You will be held accountable for what you say. This goes for guys and girls. So do like it says in Psalm 34:13: "keep your tongue from evil and your lips from speaking lies."

Lookadoo

Last Updated:
July 31, 2007

Send Message
Instant Message
Email to a Friend
Subscribe
Invite to My Blog

Gender: Male
Status: Married
Age: 101
Sign: Pisces

City: McKinney
State: TEXAS
Country: US

Signup Date:
02/17/06

Tuesday, June 12, 2007

#64 Why do girls hide their feelings, emotions, and problems and then expect us to "read their minds" and know what's wrong?

Girls think alike, and that's exactly how they operate with each other. They totally know what the other girl is feeling, and even if they don't, they can understand how emotionally draining and horrible her problem is. That's just what they do. They think alike, they talk alike, and they find comfort in the fact that someone knows them without them having to explain everything.

And for a girl who is with a guy, if they talk a lot and he knows her thoughts and moods, then she feels they have a deep cosmic connection. "Oh, it was meant to be." "He knows me." "He gets me and really likes me."

Now, guys, you can learn how to be more connected and understanding. You will never totally be there, but there are some things you can do to improve these skills.

* **Notice things:** Notice if she has lost weight or changed her hair or bought a new outfit. This is tough on a guy, but to make it easier, when she talks, listen. Has she ever said anything about trying any of these things? Lock it in your memory and ask her about it.

* **Say something:** If you know she is trying to do something or wants to, then call her on it. It's not enough just to notice. You have to say something. "Have you lost weight?" "Did you change your hair?" It is better to try it and miss than it is to have her do something and you miss the opportunity to notice. And it is so easy to recover if you are wrong. Watch this. "Did you change your hair?" "No." "Well, it sure looks good." You were wrong about the hair and you still left her

with a compliment. She won't care if you were wrong. She will think you are observant and will give you double points for the compliment save.

I am learning to do this better and better. Emily is a chocoholic. Any others out there? Yeah, you wiping the chocolate mustache off your face, she's like you. And there have been sooooooo many times that she has snapped into cocoa-monster mode late at night. And I had to make a choice: make my new wife happy or listen to her whine all night. I always chose to make her happy, and I would get up and go get her what she wanted. But now things have changed. I keep hidden stashes all over the place. Now when she starts jonesing for a fix, she knows that I have something hidden. And when I do, it makes her feel like I know her and understand her. Listen, I really don't think I know and understand her, but I know and understand that I really don't want to have to keep going to the store. Hey, we are both happy.

So fellas, pay attention to what the girl says and just make an effort to give her what she needs. In fact, the verse that I force myself to keep in my head is Philippians 2:3: "Do nothing out of selfish ambition or vain conceit, but in humility consider others better than yourselves." If I can play it like that, I am on the way to treating everyone, especially Emily, the way God wants me to treat them.

6:20 PM - 6 comments - 15 Kudos - Add Comment

Did you know?

Justin can't roll his tongue.
Or whistle.

Subject: RE: #65 What is the worst thing you can say to a girl?
Date: Tuesday, October 31, 2006 10:37 PM
From: Live conference
To: 'Justin Lookadoo' <emily@Lookadoo.com>
Conversation: Superheroes

1. You like her sister.

2. That you need her advice on how to ask *another* girl to prom.

3. "Yuck! What did you do to your hair?"

Never, ever throw out any negative comment about her body. Her zit, her makeup, her clothes, anything. If you have been going out several months—that means more than six—then you can call her attention to something embarrassing. Otherwise, if you are not her husband or friend, you don't say anything.

Here's what I'm talking about. If she has a hanger just dangling there out of her nose, you don't say anything. Let her figure it out. If she goes to the restroom and sees it in the mirror, she will be horrified, but she'll get over it. She will not get over it if you point it out.

Always choose your words carefully. Don't just throw them around, even if you are joking. Build her up with everything you do and say instead of letting your actions and words tear her down. "Do not let any unwholesome talk come out of your mouths, but only what is helpful for building others up according to their needs, that it may benefit those who listen" (Ephesians 4:29).

jlook

Lookadoo

Last Updated:
July 31, 2007

Send Message
Instant Message
Email to a Friend
Subscribe
Invite to My Blog

Gender: Male
Status: Married
Age: 101
Sign: Pisces

City: McKinney
State: TEXAS
Country: US

Signup Date:
02/17/06

Saturday, April 21, 2007

#66 What do girls look for in a guy? They always seem to pick the wrong ones. They say they want honesty, trust, and attention, but they never get what they say they are looking for.

They do want those things. But the problem comes when the guy totally focuses on giving that to her all the time. Then it's total overkill.

She wants total honesty. She wants to know all about you. But she doesn't want it all at one time. Give her some time to take a breath and process the honesty you give her.

She wants trust, but guess what? She can't grow trust if you are always around doing stuff for her and totally focused on her. You have to go away and get out of her face so she can feel that trust she's building.

She wants attention. She doesn't want false flattery but true attention. She doesn't want you to compliment her and then do it again and again and again and again and again. Yeah, you are getting annoyed with the "and again," and that is exactly how she feels when you just keep letting the compliments flow. It's almost like that whole crying wolf thing. If you do it over and over, after a while she won't believe you.

But don't let that be an excuse for not paying attention to her. Check it out. If your girl has beautiful eyes and you want to tell her, then tell her. But don't tell her every time you see her. Don't keep harping on the fact that she has beautiful eyes. Pretty soon she will be like, "I get it already!"

And let's take it a step further. Girls look for a guy who has a life. They want to be involved in something exciting. A lot of affairs or cheating happen because some other dude has the stuff she's looking for and then to top it off they have some cool stuff going on in their life. They have an excitement, a passion about life. They are caught up in something that excites them, and that excites her.

Let me give you a warning here. If your life, passion, and excitement is playing video games, fellas, you'd better understand this—you are not attractive. I mean, think about it. Which dude do you think girls would rather hang out with? The guy who spent all Christmas break sitting on his g-ma's couch wearing that knitted sweater with the little dingle-balls on the front of it and playing video games? Or do you think she would rather talk to the guy who over Christmas break went down to South America and canoed down the river taking medicine to the indigenous people? That's who I would rather talk to. He has a life. He has something going on.

Guys, dive into life. Be bold. Be strong. Check this out.

Be strong and courageous.
    (Deuteronomy 31:6)

Be strong and courageous.
    (Deuteronomy 31:7)

Be strong and courageous.
    (Deuteronomy 31:23)

Be strong and courageous.
    (Joshua 1:6)

Be strong and very courageous. Be careful to obey all the law my servant Moses gave you; do not turn from it to the right or to the left, that you may be successful wherever you go.
    (Joshua 1:7)

Be strong and courageous. Do not be terrified; do not be discouraged, for the LORD your God will be with you wherever you go.
    (Joshua 1:9)

Only be strong and courageous!
  (Joshua 1:18)

Be strong and courageous.
  (Joshua 10:25)

Be strong and brave.
  (2 Samuel 2:7)

Be strong and let us fight bravely.
  (2 Samuel 10:12)

Be strong, show yourself a man.
  (1 Kings 2:2)

Are you feeling the vibe of what God is saying here? Everything here is about shaking guys up. A coach doesn't give his team a huge pep talk if they are not going to play a game. He does it when he is trying to get his guys ready for the fight, the battle. All of these verses are focused on getting guys ready to dive off into life full-on. No fear. No regrets. On a mission with a purpose.

<u>4:50 PM</u> - <u>7 comments</u> - <u>13 Kudos</u> - <u>Add Comment</u>

Did you know?

Justin has taken several mission trips to Belize, Central America. While there he ran into the prime minister. I mean, he literally ran into him while he was snooping around the capital after hours.

Subject: RE: #67 **Why do guys think girls kissing other girls is hot?**
Date: Wednesday, March 28, 2007 1:12 AM
From: Live conference
To: 'Justin Lookadoo' <emily@Lookadoo.com>
Conversation: Superheroes

HA! I LOVE THAT. WORK IT INTO LIVE PERFORMANCE.

There's an old joke . . .

This guy is sitting beside this woman. They talk and seem to be hitting it off. The dude looks at her and says, "Would you have sex with me for a million dollars?" She thinks for a minute and says, "Yes." He then asks, "Would you have sex with me for a dollar?" She shouts, "Absolutely not! What kind of girl do you think I am?" He replies, "We've already established that. Now we're just negotiating the price."

Let me take you into the simple workings of the guy mind.

If a dude sees two girls kissing, in his mind it's settled that these girls are easy. Bonus. Plus there is no other dude, so no competition. Double bonus. And since there are two girls, his chances are twice as good. Triple bonus.

Yes, girls kissing will attract attention. But understand this, ladies. The guys this attracts don't care who you are! They just care that:

1. You're easy
2. No guy competition
3. His chances are twice as good
4. If you reject him, no worries—it's because you're a lesbian

jlook

Why are guys obsessed with boobs?

My question is, why are *girls* so obsessed with boobs? I think girls are way more obsessed with boobs than guys are. It's almost like her life and wardrobe revolve around it. Everything is "Are my breasts too small?" "Do they look too big?" "Does this shirt make them look good?" "Does it make them look too flat?" Hey, even if these Q's aren't said out loud, they definitely go through a girl's mind.

Back to the guys. I think breasts get equal attention and affection as a girl's butt, legs, abs, and whatever else. But when a guy is trying to look at a girl's face and talk to her, her breasts are right there. Now, yes, I am sure we could get into a lot of psychobabble about it being a mother issue or that guys don't have them so they are excited by them. Hey, I'm not the head doctor. I'm pretty basic. We like them. They are there. Guys are visual. And girls show them.

Does breast size really matter to a guy?

Not really. Breast preference is really a point of comparison. That's why porn is destroying young men. The point of reference that is found in pornography doesn't exist in the real world. The girl and everything she is willing to do are fake.

For the most part the thing that has the most influence on guys' preference comes from who they grew up around. Mom, granny, sisters. Not in some icky perv way. But the ladies a guy grows up with just kinda seem normal.

Don't let me lie here. Girls with big breasts who show them off will get more guy attention, and guys will seem to like those girls more. But we don't. In fact, a lot of the time guys don't like these girls at all. They just like looking at what the girl is showing. So if you are showing off your breasts, you don't really know if a dude likes you or just likes the free peek.

When a guy likes you, ladies, your breasts could be huge, small, medium, we really don't care. You will be perfect for us. Girls, read that over and over and over until you believe it, because that's the truth.

Subject: RE: #70 What should girls NOT talk about in front of guys?

Too MUCH TO MENTION!

Date: Thursday, April 26, 2007 11:45 AM
From: Live conference
To: 'Justin Lookadoo' <emily@Lookadoo.com>
Conversation: Superheroes

1. Anything "female" related. We don't need to hear about your period cycle, yeast infections, bloating, or anything else like that. Leave us with some mystery. Let us always have a fairy-tale image of you in our minds.

   PLEASE No!

2. Other girls. This catty, back-stabbing, make-other-girls-look-bad chit-chat—cut it. It doesn't work the way you think. It doesn't make us turn against the object of your wrath. It actually just makes us annoyed with you. Listen, we wouldn't hang around guys who always did that stuff, so why would we want to hang out with girls who do?

3. Your weight. Girls, don't go on and on about you being too fat or needing to lose weight or about your thighs or butt. Okay, you may really believe that or you may be fishing for compliments, but either way, it gets old quick.

If you need a compliment, don't give us a hint. We won't catch it. Throw us a bone and tell us what you need. It won't mean you're insecure. It will mean that you are smart enough to understand that guys don't take hints. That's just not our first nature. If you remind us, we'll eventually get it. We think you are beautiful. Sometimes we just forget about saying it.

Another little thing to think about. If you keep telling us how horrible you look or how fat and ugly you feel, one day you might talk us into it. Not because we think so but because we heard you say it so much that we finally believe you.

Girls, those are the three biggies. If you can steer clear of those, you will be way ahead of the crush game.

P.S.: Remember this stuff when you get married. Trust me, it doesn't change!

jlook

Justin Lookadoo
See what is happening at www.Lookadoo.com

Guys Section:
Add List of
Quick Compliments they
Can use that are Sincere
& not way cheesy!

Sunday, February 18, 2007

#71 What is the biggest thing you'd warn guys about when it comes to girls?

A girl's self-esteem is fragile and delicate. You have to watch what you say and do because it will have a long-term effect on them. The Good News Translation of the Bible puts it perfectly in Proverbs 15:4: "Kind words bring life, but cruel words crush your spirit." Bring them life, guys. Don't do or say things that will crush their spirit.

Girls will act a little crazy and irrational at times. Guys, understand that probably 80 percent of what they say right now, they really don't mean. Well, they mean it in the moment, but that will change pretty quick because they talk about the way they feel, and those feelings change. If you are pretty confused right now, great. You are understanding what I am talking about.

Beat them to the punch with compliments. If you know that she thinks she is fat (which most girls do), then tell her she is beautiful before she goes into her self-esteem beat-down. Don't wait for her to say, "Oh, I am so fat," before you tell her she looks great. I mean, that's better than nothing, but if you cut it off before she says anything, it is a lot more believable to her. And a lot more beneficial to you.

Oh, and one more thing. Don't expect any good explanations for her tears or actions. They won't make sense anyway. And the one you get may not be the real deal.

Confusing? Yes. But girls are one of the most intriguing, exciting creatures God ever made. If you learn how to interact, listen, be there for her, and build her up, you will see her grow and blossom into a beautiful reflection of God.

8:09 AM - **9 comments** - **7 Kudos** - **Add Comment**

Lookadoo

Last Updated:
July 31, 2007

Send Message
Instant Message
Email to a Friend
Subscribe
Invite to My Blog

Gender: Male
Status: Married
Age: 101
Sign: Pisces

City: McKinney
State: TEXAS
Country: US

Signup Date:
02/17/06

Friday, October 20, 2006

#72 What is the biggest thing you would warn us girls about when it comes to guys?

Guys need you to let them win. Don't challenge them on everything. Yes, we love a challenge, but you have to let us win and catch you. We want to be that guy every once in a while. See, if you challenge a guy on everything, then he will try to impress you more, so he will do even more stupid things. It's a bad domino effect. Let the guy know that he *does* impress you before he gets super stupid.

11:48 AM - 5 comments - 8 Kudos - Add Comment

DID YOU KNOW? EMILY HAS OVER 700 SKYDIVES. SHE HAS BEEN CLOCKED GOING 217 MPH.

Lookadoo

Last Updated:
July 31, 2007

Send Message
Instant Message
Email to a Friend
Subscribe
Invite to My Blog

Gender: Male
Status: Married
Age: 101
Sign: Pisces

City: McKinney
State: TEXAS
Country: US

Signup Date:
02/17/06

Tuesday, May 8, 2007

#73 Is it true that if you want to know what a guy is really like, you should watch how he treats his mother?

No. Do not watch the way he treats his mother, for the most part. Watch how he treats someone who can do nothing for him. Watch how he treats the waiter who keeps getting stuff wrong. Listen to what he says about the janitor at school. If you want to know what someone is really like, pay attention to what they do for and say about people who can do nothing for them and who they are not trying to impress. Because guess what? Sooner than you think, this person will snap out of that "trying to impress you" mode, and that's exactly how they will treat you.

If you want to look inside the family, then look at how the father treats the mother. If they are not together, still look at that. This dude will see how this interaction happens, and that will be his only pattern for how to treat a lady. If they are divorced and dad is always trashing mom, guess what, ladies? That is his model. If dad is always caring for, protecting, honoring, and praising mom, then guess what, ladies? That is his model. If it's only mom around and no male role models have helped raise this dude, then it's a crapshoot. You don't know what you'll end up with. You have to keep an eye on the sitch and see how things are going.

3:08 PM – 6 comments – 14 Kudos – Add Comment

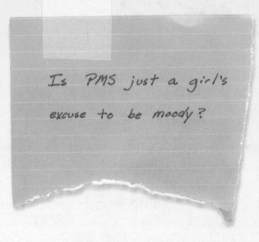

Is PMS just a girl's excuse to be moody?

Nope. That's a guy's excuse. That is what we blame for any bad day, bad moment, or just about anything we don't understand about girls.

Did you know Justin broke his toe when he kicked the stairs while arguing with Emily.

Tue, July 31, 2007 9:43 PM

Subject: RE: #75 Why does a guy tell you one thing and then do something that seems to totally contradict what he said?

Date: Friday, June 1, 2007 9:24 AM

From: Live conference

To: 'Justin Lookadoo' <emily@Lookadoo.com>

Conversation: Superheroes

duh!

One reason could be that *he's a guy*. He is telling you one thing because he wants to win the game and get you to like him. Then he tells his boys another thing because he is trying to win *that* game and get them to think he's cool.

double duh!

The other reason could be because *he's a guy*. And when a guy tells you something, ladies, he means it. He just doesn't mean it like you take it.

When a guy says he wants to be with you forever, ladies, you think he means . . . *forever*. Well, he means it; he just doesn't mean it like that. A guy's concept of time is different than a girl's. Forever? Yeah, next Friday could seem like forever.

For more on this go get my book *97: Random Thoughts about Life, Love, and Relationships* and check out #67.

jlook

Justin Lookadoo
Check out Justin's bestselling book
Dateable: are you? are they?

If they have more questions send them to www.lookadoo.com Chat section.

Things To Do:

☐
☐ Why do my ex-
☐ boyfriends always
☐ date ugly girls?
☐
☐
☐
☐
☐
☐
☐
☐
☐
☐
☐
☐

Because no one could *ever* measure up to you.

Subject: RE: #77 Why will guys say they like you and that you're hot but not date you?
Date: Saturday, July 22, 2007 6:28 PM
From: Live conference
To: 'Justin Lookadoo' <emily@Lookadoo.com>
Conversation: Superheroes

Uh . . . because they like you and think you're hot but they don't want to date you. Believe it or not, ladies, guys can actually be like that. They can think you are hot without wanting to date you.

jlook

Justin Lookadoo
Order your copy of the
*3-part Dateable DVD **now!*** *product@lookadoo.com*

Did you know? Before Emily met Justin he spotted her from two restaurants away. He watched her several times. He called it love. The police called it stalking.

Lookadoo

Last Updated:
July 31, 2007

Send Message
Instant Message
Email to a Friend
Subscribe
Invite to My Blog

Gender: Male
Status: Married
Age: 101
Sign: Pisces

City: McKinney
State: TEXAS
Country: US

Signup Date:
02/17/06

Tuesday, April 17, 2007

#78 Why do guys only start talking to a girl when they want to date her?

Guys love a challenge. They love the game. So if they start chatting up a girl who is attached to someone or who they don't want to go out with, they are jumping into a game that doesn't have an end. What's the point? If they cannot even live a little fantasy in their minds that there is a possibility, then they probably won't even start.

I'm not telling you this is right or wrong; I'm just telling you that's the way it is.

8:12 AM – **13 comments** – **8 Kudos** - **Add Comment**

About | FAQ | **Terms** | **Privacy** | **Safety Tips** | **Chat Room** | **97** | **Shop**

Why do guys leave the toilet seat up?

My question is, why can't girls handle this one? Okay, get the visual. For a guy, we have to bend over, lift the seat, and then we have to bend over to put it back down. Doesn't it make more sense that when a girl sits down, she reaches out and takes the toilet seat with her? I mean, she's going that direction anyway. And then when she stands, she just lifts the seat as she stands. Makes sense to me. Go to <u>www.lookadoo .com</u> and let me know what you think about that.

Subject: RE: #80 Why do guys think girls like them even when they don't?
Date: Saturday, September 16, 2006 12:38 AM
From: Live conference
To: 'Justin Lookadoo' <emily@Lookadoo.com>
Conversation: Superheroes

This is all about a guy's ego. Hey, if I am walking down the hall with my boys, and a girl even looks in my direction, yeah, she wants me. The truth is irrelevant. It's all about our ego. It's a short jump from us thinking she *should* like us to convincing ourselves that she really does.

jlook

Justin Lookadoo
Check out Justin's bestselling book *Dateable: are you? are they?*

Subject: RE: #81 Why do guys feel like they have to prove their masculinity?

Date: Thursday, May 31, 2007 1:49 PM

From: Live conference

To: 'Justin Lookadoo' <emily@Lookadoo.com>

Conversation: Superheroes

Guys who haven't settled this become Angry & Aggressive.

Because guys have to prove their masculinity. The way it is designed is that we are supposed to prove it by having strong, godly men push us to do things we didn't think we could. But a lot of times that doesn't happen. So guys have to find other ways to try to figure out if we have what it takes to be a man.

Then if you put in the hormonal influence of trying to prove to girls that we are real men, oh, wow, it really gets messed up. But understand that guys have to test their manhood. It's just that we do it in some really stupid ways sometimes.

jlook

Justin Lookadoo

Buy Justin's hit new release **97**

Parenting Conf:
① MALE ROLE ✗ MOTHER
② FEMAL ROLE ✗ FATHER

- - - - - - - - - - - - - - - -

Did you know? Justin won the title of "best model" in his first 4-H sewing competition and fashion show.

Monday, February 5, 2007

#82 Why do guys expect girls to make the first move?

Because guys are lazy. And girls, you have taught guys that the easiest way for us to get a girl is to hand out our phone number to a whole bunch of girls and then go home, play video games, and wait for you to call. And guess what, ladies—you will. Every time. We really don't even wait to see *if* you call; we wait to see in what order you call.

Ladies, you want to change the game on a guy? The next time a guy hands you a phone number to call him, you slide it back with your number and say, "Here, if you want to do something, you call me."

Guess what, ladies—we will. If we like you, we will do anything. And if he doesn't call you, then understand that either he doesn't like you enough to put in any effort or he is not ready to ask you out. Either way, you don't want him.

7:30 PM - **2 comments** - **1 Kudos** - **Add Comment**

Tue, July 31, 2007 9:47 PM

Subject: RE: #83 Why do guys have to act so tough when they get hurt?

Date: Friday, November 3, 2006 10:09 PM

From: Live conference

To: 'Justin Lookadoo' <emily@Lookadoo.com>

Conversation: Superheroes

We could go into a lot of psychological yuckity-yuck about why this happens, and I am sure that a lot of it is true. But I think it has a lot to do with finding out if the boy has what it takes to be a man. And this is just one of those tests that guys put on themselves. You've seen it even in little boys. They get hurt and their eyes start to get tears, and they want to cry but they fight it. This even happens when no one is telling them not to cry. From a young age guys have a need to know that we are tough and that we can take care of business and be a man.

jlook

Handwritten: Don't go too deep ON THIS ONE

Justin Lookadoo

See what is happening at www.Lookadoo.com

Did you know? Justin broke one wrist, cracked the other, and busted his chin wide open while slam-dunking a basketball . . . in pregame warmup.

Do girls like the sensitive guy or the tough guy?

Yes. She likes the tough sensitive guy. She likes the guy who is strong enough to take care of her yet sensitive enough to listen and understand her. Go get *Dateable: Are You? Are They?* and check out the sections about how to stand up and be a man.

Girls don't want a jerk, but they don't want a pansy. They want something in the middle . . . a jerpansy.

Wardrobe Malfunctions

[fashion dos and don'ts]

Did you KNOW?

Justin and Emily had a vintage wedding. It was a double-knit polyester explosion.

Wednesday, November 22, 2006

#85 Why do girls dress in tight, skimpy clothes and then freak out when guys look?

They don't. Okay, maybe they freak out, but not because they *are* freaked out. It's about attention. When girls dress that way, they are trying to attract attention. If they get it by making someone stare and then flip about it, it's because they are trying to grab even more attention.

And for the girls reading this thinking, *No, I don't. That's not why I get upset,* fine. But let me ask you this. What if that hot guy you've been crushing on forever was staring at your body—would you freak out? No. Of course not. Because you would be flattered that he noticed you. But you get mad when the guys you don't like or don't even know start gawking at you. Girls, you can't have it all. You can't dress so that a certain guy will notice your body and then get mad when *every* guy stares at your goods. You can't tell the ugly guy to keep his eyes off because you know what he's thinking and it grosses you out and then get all bubbly when the guy you like does the exact same thing.

Girls can dress trashy for some other reasons too.

Some girls really have little or no fashion sense. They just buy stuff that they think looks good on someone else, and they never take into consideration their own body type, size, shape, and so on. And they end up in some clothes they shouldn't because they don't realize it makes them look the way they do.

Some girls are trying to boost their self-esteem, and somehow they have come to believe that the higher the hemline, the higher the self-esteem. But they don't realize that the attention they are getting is actually tearing them down even more.

Girls know people are looking. They know when what they show will attract attention. But most don't realize the sin that goes with it. They don't realize that they are responsible for the thoughts of guys when they are showing their flesh. I often quote 1 Timothy 2:9, "I also want women to dress modestly, with decency and propriety," and most of you understand this. For those of you who just blow by this verse, let me give you another one: "Therefore let us stop passing judgment on one another. Instead, make up your mind not to put any stumbling block or obstacle in your brother's way" (Romans 14:13). Causing a stumbling block is exactly what you are doing if you are showing off your bod with the revealing threads.

1:15 AM - 7 comments - 12 Kudos - Add Comment

Did you know?

Justin was crowned Powder-Puff Queen while he was in college.

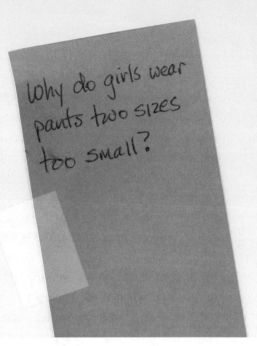

Why do girls wear pants two sizes too small?

Because 5 and 7 are good sizes. You heard me. Girls have been taught that size matters when you're talking about your clothes. They don't want to admit that they really wear a 9. Or if they really wear an 11 they will buy the 9 so they don't have to own up to the 11. It's not really about the guys. It's about admitting it to themselves and to other girls.

See, when another girl looks at her clothes and says, "That is sooooo cute. What size is it?" she doesn't want to lie. She would rather say, "I dunno," or at least be able to say something that sounds smaller than the truth.

Measurements have been in our lives from the beginning. Every time we go to the nurse or gym we see the height/weight charts, and girls have it pounded into their mentals that at 5 foot you should be 100 pounds and it goes up 5 pounds per inch. They know that an hourglass figure means a

10-inch difference from bust to waist to hips and pear-shaped is not acceptable.

Every girl knows that when her friends are in her room, they are checking out the sizes in her clothes. How does she know? Because she's doing the same thing. Oh, and the major gauge of beauty is to find a girl you think is pretty and find out her weight and size of clothes. Then if you can make yourself fit in her size, you can convince yourself that you are pretty.

I know, you guys are going cross-eyed now thinking, *Why did I ask that question?* But just hang in there. This is the real deal.

Another big reason for the way girls dress is the fact that they are growing up. And when that happens you want everyone to know. You want people to recognize that you are changing. Then nature throws a dirty trick in the hormonal potion and you start breaking out in a bumper crop of zits. Your skin goes crazy, and you look in the mirror and wonder who that goofazoid is looking back at you, and you would rather have people stare at anything other than your face. It is so much easier to dress with tight pants and low-cut shirts so people, especially guys, will see the sex in your clothes and not the hex on your nose.

Girls, if you don't like the way you look, you need to do something about it if you can. I am 6 foot 7. I can't change that, so I had to learn to deal with being tall. Accept the stuff about you that you can't change. But if you hate the fact that you are overweight, then don't just say, "This is the way God made me." No, if you just sit on the couch eating marshmallows and carrot cake, that is not the way God made you. Do something about it. I know someone asked about this stuff somewhere else in this book. Go find the question about how weight affects relationships.

We got a little off the topic here, but girls, dress in clothes that fit you. If you want, rip all the tags off your clothes. That way when someone says, "What size is that?" you can just shrug and say, "Check the tag."

Know that you were made beautiful and you were designed. Not by accident but by a God who cares. "For you created my inmost being; you knit me together in my mother's womb. I praise you because I am fearfully and wonderfully made; your works are wonderful, I know that full well. My frame was not hidden from you when I was made in the secret place. When I was woven together in the depths of the earth, your eyes saw my unformed body. All the days ordained for me were written in your book before one of them came to be" (Psalm 139:13–16).

Guy Tip: Guys, never say anything except good stuff about her appearance. Nothing about her zits, boogers, smells, or anything you would normally make fun of your guy friends about. It won't get you a good reaction, and she won't forget it.

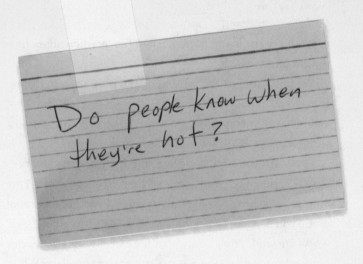

Do people know when they're hot?

Yes, and usually they'll turn on the air conditioner.

Did you know when Justin started skydiving, he had to wear his wife's pants.

Lookadoo

Last Updated:
July 31, 2007

Send Message
Instant Message
Email to a Friend
Subscribe
Invite to My Blog

Gender: Male
Status: Married
Age: 101
Sign: Pisces

City: McKinney
State: TEXAS
Country: US

Signup Date:
02/17/06

Thursday, May 10, 2007

#88 What do Christian guys think about girls wearing a lot of makeup?

They don't like it. And this really isn't a *Christian* guy thing. It's a *guy* thing. They want to see you, not a mask that you hide behind. And most guys think that girls that wear a lot of makeup are insecure.

Now don't get me wrong. I'm not saying we hate makeup. In fact, most guys say they like girls who don't wear makeup because they don't realize the girl they are hot for is actually wearing some. We don't mind makeup. We just don't like a girl to look like she has any on.

A couple of hints: If your face is a different color than your arms . . . too much. If you have a definite line where the makeup ends and your neck begins . . . too much. If you sweat and your face streaks like water running down a muddy windshield . . . too much. If we see you with makeup and then see you without it and we don't recognize who you are . . . too much.

We want to see the real you. A little cover-up, eye color, and lip liner, it's all good. But when we hug you, we don't want to wear part of your face on our shirt.

It seems like a lot of girls spend way more time looking in the mirror trying to cover up who they are than they do spending time with God discovering who they really are.

—John Charles Colclasure

Clowns are allowed to wear a lot of makeup. Are you a clown?

6:32 PM - **8 comments** - **1 Kudos** - **Add Comment**

Subject: RE: #89 My mom won't let me wear clothes that show my tummy. How can I get her to chill out?
Date: Tuesday, December 5, 2006 6:27 AM
From: Live conference
To: 'Justin Lookadoo' <emily@Lookadoo.com>
Conversation: Wardrobe Malfunctions

Captain OBVIOUS SAYS:

By not wearing clothes that show your tummy!

Your mom doesn't want you to wear those clothes because she knows you are beautiful and the skimpy clothes make you look easy. Your dad doesn't want you to wear skimpy clothes because he knows that when you do, guys are thinking about you in your revealing clothes, and then they are thinking about what you'll do with them without those clothes. And girls, that's exactly what is happening.

1 Tim 2:9 ck this verse.

Ladies, check out what it says in 1 Timothy 2:9: "I also want women to dress modestly, with decency and propriety, not with braided hair or gold or pearls or expensive clothes." Don't get hung up on the braided hair, gold, pearls, and stuff. Back in the day, that was what the ladies did to get all sexy. Today it could be translated as "not in your tight little spaghetti-strap half-shirt with your skintight low-rise pants showing off all your business."

So if you want to get your parents to chill, then don't wear it. And for those who want to argue, don't make me whip out Colossians 3:20: "Children, obey your parents in everything, for this pleases the Lord."

jlook

Subject: RE: #90 Does Jesus really love me and my tattoos and piercings?
Date: Thursday, January 25, 2007 3:29 PM
From: Live conference
To: 'Justin Lookadoo' <emily@Lookadoo.com>
Conversation: Wardrobe Malfunctions

[handwritten: Just talked to a guy in Atlanta who wants info about the evils of tatoos]

This stuff has nothing to do with God's love. I don't care who says what about it. You have to go back to the Bible. Romans 8:39 says, "Neither height nor depth, nor anything else in all creation, will be able to separate us from the love of God that is in Christ Jesus our Lord." That means tattoos, piercings, hair, music—nothing can separate you from the love of God. And not just the love of God but also the connection that comes from following Christ as your Savior and guide.

[handwritten: Bear Tat]

As for the people out there who shout that tats are straight from hell and are totally against God's Word, well, they typically quote Leviticus chapter 19 verse 28: "Do not cut your bodies for the dead or put tattoo marks on yourselves. I am the LORD." First of all, this is directed especially at putting tattoo marks on yourself for the dead. This was a form of paganism and idolatry. But then we have to break it down even further. If you are going to totally accept this as the "you are a sinner" verse against tattoos, you have to read everything in this section of Leviticus. Check this out, verse 19: "Do not wear clothing woven of two kinds of material." Check your tags and if you have a cotton-poly blend, oops, you're going against God. Or verse 27: "Do not cut the hair at the sides of your head or clip off the edges of

You can't pick & CHOOSE!

your beard." Wait a minute. Have you had a haircut or shaved? You're a sinner. And in verse 32 it says, "Rise in the presence of the aged, show respect for the elderly." Have you ever had an older person walk into the room and you didn't stand up? There you go again . . . sinner. I am sure the people who use verse 28 to condemn you for your tattoos would have an excuse for why those other verses are irrelevant but verse 28 still condemns you. Either way, don't worry about God's love. He loves you and you can't change that.

So what is the issue here? Well, first there is probably a parent issue. If you are still under your parents' roof and you are not paying your own way in life, then it is very important to know Ephesians 6:1-3: "Children, obey your parents in the Lord, for this is right. 'Honor your father and mother'—which is the first commandment with a promise—'that it may go well with you and that you may enjoy long life on the earth.'" That means if you want piercings and tats but your parentals say no, then that's what you go with. If you do it anyway, then think about the opposite of that verse. Don't honor your father and mother and it may *not* go well with you and you may not enjoy a long life. Honor them . . . joy. Not honor them . . . probably not. So if they are against your ink or holes all over your bod, honor them and don't do it, especially while you are living in their house with their support. Once you get out doing your own thing you are in a better spot to make that call.

Now for the big issue. This is the question you ask yourself before you do anything—relationships, jobs, tat, whatever. Ask yourself, "Is it holy?" The truth

Is it Holy

is, most things aren't holy when there's an audience. Check it. If you rip off your shirt and say, "Check this out," it has probably lost its holiness. If you wear shirts that show off what you have pierced, my guess is the answer may be no, it's not holy. Even praying can be unholy. If you are praying before your meal and you go on and on and on while the waiter is standing there breaking his back, I would imagine it has lost its holiness. Likewise, if you pray so loud that the entire restaurant has to shut up because you are praying, I bet it's not holy. Something that you do for spectators loses its holiness.

If you are at that restaurant and you choose to pray quietly and people take notice, hey, that wasn't your intention. That made an impression on others without you trying to do it. If you have a tattoo, someone asks about it, you get to tell them the story behind the tat, and it points to Christ, hey, that is totally holy.

Just to finish this out and make sure we are all on the same level:

1. You can't do anything to knock you out of God's love. Those who follow Christ are always loved.

2. If you are living with the parentals and they don't agree with it, then the biblical answer to your wanting tats and piercings is no.

3. Ask yourself, "Is it holy?" Are you doing something that will permanently mark you for your glory or God's?

jlook

Did you KNOW?

When Emly was growing up. her dad made her wear a shower cap at the dinner table because she was so messy.

God Talk

[questions about faith]

Thursday, March 8, 2007

#91 When you speak, why do you seem to tell a lot of stories and only use a little bit of Scripture?

Yeah, I get that quite a bit, and you are right. I do that.

Actually, I pattern my speaking style after a friend of mine. He would tell stories that would connect with people, and then he would hit them with the Scripture. He seemed to be pretty effective. In fact, you may have read some of his stuff. Yeah, some of it was published in the New Testament. His name is Jesus.

Jesus didn't stand up and start spouting off Scripture and then try to tell people what it meant. He would come with stories and illustrations, and he would weave a tale. Then at the right moment, he would ping them with the Word. That's what I try to do.

Now, I'm not downing guys that go through a thousand Scriptures and break them down. They are Bible teachers, and I love listening to them. That's not my calling, though. I'm called to use my gifts, style, and abilities the best I can. That's what we are all called to do. Even you.

2:18 PM - 9 comments - 13 Kudos - Add Comment

Did you know?

Emily was a painter.

Subject: RE: #92 Do you ever feel intimidated by people who don't believe in God?
Date: Thursday, March 22, 2007 3:45 AM
From: Live conference
To: 'Justin Lookadoo' <emily@Lookadoo.com>
Conversation: God Talk

Yes and no. I'm not intimidated just because of someone's beliefs. I get intimidated when I have to talk about what I believe in an intellectual way. See, I think that most of us as Christians don't know how to talk intellectually about why we believe what we believe. In fact, I heard someone say one time that if you ask an average Christian "Why?" three times, you will rock the foundation of their faith.

"Why are you a Christian?"

"Because I follow Christ."

"Why?"

"Because that's what I believe."

"Why?"

"Because that's what the Bible says."

"Why?"

"Uhhh . . ."

See, we get intimidated because we can't back up why we believe what we believe. It's all emotional. Not that emotions are bad. But they don't work if that's all you've got.

"Why do you follow Christ?"

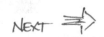

"Because that's what I believe." Great. People who strap bombs to themselves and walk into the middle of the market think they get a first-class ticket to the afterlife. And...

"Because it changed my life." Great. Every person devoted to Satan worship has had a life-changing experience too. And...

Hey, I'm not downing your experience. No one can take that away from you. But my point is that if you are going to be an intensely effective Christian, you need to know why you believe the Bible is true, and I am sorry to say that this issue is way too big for us to cover here. But let me give you a few things that will help you get going.

This is a must. Get one for everyone in the office.

The book *The Case for Christ* by Lee Strobel is something you have to get. I think it should be a must-read for everyone who is a Christian. Lee was a legal reporter in Chicago and used those investigative skills to research Christ. Basically he was going to disprove the four Gospels. If you do that, then the rest of the Christian faith crumbles. Through his research he meticulously proves the case for Christ. This book will help strengthen your faith and confidence as to why you believe.

If you want to bump it up a notch, then check out *Evidence that Demands a Verdict* by Josh McDowell. This goes even deeper and even more toward the intellectual vibe of the history and truth of Christ.

I'm not saying that you are not a true Christian if you believe simply because you believe and you don't really know why. But if you are going to become a powerful warrior, unshaken and not intimidated by different beliefs, you need to know the evidence that builds the foundation for your beliefs. When you know the answers, you start to welcome the questions. You don't run from them.

I am on the same journey now. So if you are ready for the challenge, then jump in and we can ride this one together. Not just so people will think we sound cool but so we can do what the Word tells us when it says, "But in your hearts set apart Christ as Lord. Always be prepared to give an answer to everyone who asks you to give the reason for the hope that you have. But do this with gentleness and respect" (1 Peter 3:15).

jlook

Justin Lookadoo
Buy Justin's hit new release **97**

Go BACK & RE-READ CASE FOR CHRIST!

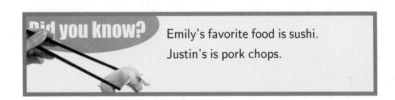

Did you know?

Emily's favorite food is sushi.
Justin's is pork chops.

Saturday, January 27, 2007

#93 The Bible says we are supposed to be salt and light. What can you tell us that would help us do that in high school?

Here, I'll give a quick list:

* 1. Get full.

* 2. Don't quote Scripture all the time.

* 3. Be confident.

Let's break all this down. I was talking with two girls in Indiana. They are sisters and they are way cool. They are beautiful, fashionable, popular, sweet, dynamic—they are the package. And they are totally sold out, high-octane followers of Christ. I have watched them for some time and noticed that they have an impact on people just by living their lives. So I asked them how they pulled it off that they are committed Christians and are still cool. Their response? "We're not empty." I asked them to explain and they told me that they are not lacking anything, so they aren't bothered by what people say about them. They live their lives and they have a blast. They have a solid connection with Christ. They know who they are because they know who the Bible says they are.

They don't get invited to the parties, and people stop their conversations about their weekends when the sisters walk up, but they don't really mind. They are the ones everyone runs to when something goes bad. They don't lash out at what people do. They don't judge them. They don't sit back and quote Scripture to everyone, and they don't wear Christian T-shirts around. They are salt. They make people thirsty to be like them.

The reason they are so confident is because they know Scripture. They are confident in their relationship with Christ without being overly churchy, and that makes them attractive. Then when someone comes up to them with a problem, they become the light. We could talk about so much more here, but I've got other questions to answer. Remember to be full of God, humble about who you are, confident about your faith and people will want what you have. And God will use you.

11:17 AM - 8 comments - 5 Kudos - Add Comment

Subject: RE: #94 When people say, "I heard the Lord say . . ." how do they know?

Date: Wednesday, January 31, 2007 1:51 PM

From: Live conference

To: 'Justin Lookadoo' <emily@Lookadoo.com>

Conversation: God Talk

It's a process. You don't wake up one morning and just "know." Let me ask you this. Is there someone who calls you and as soon as you hear their voice, you know who it is? Sure. Well, how did you get to where you knew? Think about it. I'm not giving you the answer here. You tell me. (This is me waiting . . .) How did you get to where you know their voice? If you said, "Because I talk to the person," you are wrong. If you talked to the person a lot, then they would know your voice. You wouldn't know theirs. Yeah, that was the hint of all hints for the slow people.

You have to *listen* to someone. You have to hear their voice and connect the voice with the person. That little listen and connect thing is important. Is there someone's voice that you recognize but you don't know who it is? Like you hear a song and as soon as you hear their voice, you know two other songs they sing, but you don't know who it is? Or even the voice on the old TV commercial, "Ho! Ho! Ho! Green Giant." Yeah, I recognize the voice, but I don't know who it is.

Flip it. Are there people you know but whose voice you can't recognize? Sure, there are lots of those.

So let's get all of this stuff laid out to solve this puzzle of knowing if it is God speaking. First we have to look at the normal ways God speaks to us. I know he is God and can change things anytime he wants, but he is not doing this grand game of hide-and-seek. He wants to be found. So how does that happen?

Obviously, the Bible is one of the biggies. I mean, you're reading along and something jumps out or hits you. This is the closest thing we have to a recording of God's voice. When you get into the Bible, you start picking up on the character of God. You see how he acts and what he does or says about stuff. You catch up on what God's will is, and God will never say anything against his will, which means nothing contra to the Bible.

Prayer is another huge way to hear God. And that doesn't mean you talking. God doesn't need to get to know your voice. You need to hear his. So prayer means I pick a topic. Maybe it was something I was talking to God about or maybe it's just an issue that pops in my mind. I ask God what he wants me to see or do in this sitch. Then I sit and wait in silence with a pen and paper, and I write down whatever comes to my head. And as I write it down I ask, "Is there anything else?" And I wait. When I don't sense that there is anything else, then I look at what I wrote down. I try not to ask, "Does this make sense?" because a lot of times God's words don't make logical sense. What I do ask is "Does this fit in with what the Bible says?" Because remember, God will never tell you something that goes against his Word. So, if you start coming up with stuff that goes against Scripture or isn't holy, check that you are really listening to God, not just writing down your own ideas.

Once I get to where I have searched and believe that God is telling me to do something, then I do it.

Whatever it is. That is where many people get hung up on learning the voice of God. God talks a ton, but we don't act. We really don't know if it was truly the voice of God until we act. So act. If it is the will of God, you'll know pretty quick because you will have that peace that is beyond all understanding. If it wasn't, then go back and ask again.

Just like getting to know someone's voice, the more you listen and react and connect, the more you will start hearing God's voice and know with confidence it was him. You will be led by him, and you will be able to say, "I heard the Lord say . . ." And you will know it was him without a doubt.

jlook

Justin Lookadoo
Order your copy of the
3-part Dateable DVD now! product@lookadoo.com

[handwritten note: EXPAND ON THAT & TURN INTO A PRAYER TRAINING]

Did you know? When Justin was a baby, his sister would poke him while he was sleeping and then run to their parents, exclaiming, "Uh-oh, baby cry!"

Do you ever
stray from
God?

I am sad to say it, but yes. I get into my own little world and do my own little things. It is so subtle too. It starts with me getting really busy. I don't have time for everything, so I would rather grab fifteen more minutes of sleep than wake up early and spend time with God. That moves into me slowly getting more busy to the point where I don't have time to go to church. Then I find myself getting more irritated and angry. Then I start letting my thoughts go crazy and not controlling them. Oh, it's so slow and subtle that I almost don't see that it's happening. But I am learning and growing. I am recognizing my patterns, and I am trying to stop them at the beginning before I start blowing it all.

Lookadoo

Last Updated:
July 31, 2007

Send Message
Instant Message
Email to a Friend
Subscribe
Invite to My Blog

Gender: Male
Status: Married
Age: 101
Sign: Pisces

City: McKinney
State: TEXAS
Country: US

Signup Date:
02/17/06

Monday, December 4, 2006

#96 Why do people go around saying that we are here for a purpose when other people say that everything is a test of whether we'll get to heaven?

Well, we are here for a purpose, and that is to become Christlike and to bring glory to God. And yes, everything is a test. But it's not a test to get to heaven. When you choose to give the controls of your life to God and follow Jesus, then the heaven issue is over. Jesus said, "I am the way and the truth and the life. No one comes to the Father except through me" (John 14:6). If you come to Jesus, you get to the Father. So everything else is not a test for eternity. These things are tests as well as training to help you become more like the one you say you live for.

9:30 AM - 6 comments - 12 Kudos - Add Comment

Did you know?

The two worst school subjects for Justin were reading and writing. Today he is a best-selling author.

Did you KNOW?

Justin and Emily sponsor a child in the Dominican Republic through Compassion International. They went on a Compassion trip to DR. and their lives were forever changed. If you want to make a difference, you can. The work that Compassion does is more than amazing. When you are ready to do what the Word of God has called us to do and take care of the poor, then head on over to the website www.compassion.com.

The Universe at Large
[stuff that doesn't fit anywhere else]

Did you KNOW?

Justin played a mad scientist in a multi-media show for schools.

Subject: RE: #97 If you can't read or write very well, how did you end up with a biology degree?
Date: Thursday, December 21, 2006 10:37 PM
From: Live conference
To: 'Justin Lookadoo' <emily@Lookadoo.com>
Conversation: The Universe at Large

It wasn't easy. My first semester in college I had freshman biology class, and it didn't take long for me to figure out that I was getting left behind. I wanted to do well, but I couldn't remember what I had just read in the book or what I heard in class. So I had to come up with a plan, and here's what I did:

1. I would sit in class and take notes the best I could. Meanwhile, I had a tape recorder, and I taped the class.

2. I would go home and listen to the lecture again and fill in the stuff I missed.

3. Next I would take those notes and rewrite them neatly on a yellow paper tablet using colored pens.

4. Then I would take different colored highlighters and highlight each section of info, rotating the colors.

5. I would use these notes and transfer each little sentence or bit of info onto 3-by-5 index cards.

6. Finally, I would highlight key words with the color that matched the color on the yellow paper notes.

Welcome to my World!

And at this point, I *still* didn't know the info. But now it was set up so that I could learn it. That's how I got through school.

Yuckness

Please don't tell me you can't pass your classes because you're dumb or learning disabled or ADHD or any other label people throw on you. Don't use that as an excuse. You can do it. You just may have to figure out a different way of doing things. And guess what? You may have to work really hard to succeed.

If you just read what I had to go through for my college degree and thought, *There's no way I'm gonna do that*, then don't come to me whining about not being able to pass your classes or get your promotion or whatever. If you are not willing to work at it, I'm not willing to listen to you talk about why you can't do something.

Try what I did. If it doesn't work for you, then try something else. And if that doesn't work, try something else, and keep trying until you find something that will work for you. You can do it.

jlook

Justin Lookadoo
Check out Justin's bestselling book *Dateable: are you? are they?*

Did you know? Emily cannot watch a movie where animals get hurt, die, or even walk with a limp. Justin has missed a lot of good movies because of this.

What's wrong with MySpace?

Nothing. That's like asking what's wrong with telephones, TV, email, or anything else. There's nothing really wrong with it. But there are definitely some problems with the way people use it.

Do you ever write negative or hurtful things about other people?

Do you get on other people's sites and post bad stuff?

Do you post borderline sexual, bikini-type pictures of yourself or others?

Do you go to sites with some info, pics, or content that you wouldn't want your pastor to see?

Would you change your content if you knew your parents, teachers, or pastors were looking at it? (Guess what—one of them probably is.)

Do you post or tell anyone where you live or your real phone numbers?

Do you spend five or more hours a week on this type of site?

If you answered yes to any of these, then there is definitely a problem with your usage. You need to change what you are doing because you are accountable for everything you do and for everything you write or say. "I tell you that men will have to give account on the day of judgment for every careless word they have spoken" (Matthew 12:36).

Wednesday, January 17, 2007

#99 What should you do when your friend says that you and your other friends are excluding her, but you try to hang out with her and you invite her to sit with you, and she doesn't want to? She just walks away. The girl who is feeling excluded seems like she wants attention. What should I do?

Ask yourself the big question, "What have I done that could cause her to feel bad?" Because here's the deal. The most overlooked reason that people treat you like that is because either you have done something to them or you have done something to someone else and now your reputation precedes you. So be real with yourself. Is there anything you could have possibly done or said that maybe even if taken out of context could make the person feel bad? Even if you think it's no big deal, it must have been to them. If you come up with anything, accept responsibility for it. Apologize sincerely. That means with none of this "but you did this or she said that" crap. Just apologize and then keep asking them to do stuff. They will say no, but keep asking. Be consistent and don't quit. Don't give them a reason to say, "See, I knew they were fake."

Even if you haven't done anything, someone else did, and it may take a while for them to trust you. You are battling what was done to them, even if it really wasn't you who did it. It's not easy to stick with it, but it will be so worth it.

Here's a little help on how to open up the relations. We'll start with some very important words in your question: "you and your other friends." Stop trying to get her to join your group. Apparently she doesn't trust your group. Show up at her house *alone*. Sit by her *alone*. Start a conversation with her *alone*. Get out of your group because she doesn't want to be a part of the group. Once she trusts you, then maybe you can add other people. But for now reach out to her—just you and not the gang. Check this out:

> Though I am free and belong to no man, I make myself a slave to everyone, to win as many as possible. To the Jews I became like a Jew, to win the Jews. To those under the law I became like one under the law (though I myself am not under the law), so as to win those under the law. To those not having the law I became like one not having the law (though I am not free from God's law but am under Christ's law), so as to win those not having the law. To the weak I became weak, to win the weak. I have become all things to all men so that by all possible means I might save some. I do all this for the sake of the gospel, that I may share in its blessings.
>
> 1 Corinthians 9:19–23

That pretty much seals the deal on what we're talking about. Don't try to get other people to jump into your pool; you go to where they are and be what *they* need you to be, not what you think they need.

8:03 PM - 16 comments - 3 Kudos - Add Comment

Did you know?

Before Justin was a bestselling author, he was a juvenile probation officer, air-conditioner factory worker, blizzard wizard at Dairy Queen, and horticultural home builder (hole digger).

Yeah, that is a weird deal. Check this out. The two things I am worst at in this world? Reading and writing. I am horrible at them and I hate the process. It's always been like that and it still is.

I was sitting at my house talking on the phone with a friend of mine who worked for a publisher, and he said, "Hey, I need you to write a book." I laughed. I thought he was joking. He knew I couldn't read and write very well.

We talked for a while more and he asked, "So are you gonna do it?" I said, "Are you serious?" He said, "Yep." I told him that I would have to get back to him.

I sat back in my chair and just laughed. I said, "God, you made me a speaker, not a writer. I'm going to stick with that, and I have no doubt that lives will be changed through my speaking." And I knew it was God when I heard, "You're right. Your speaking will change other people. I'm about to change *you* with your writing."

And you know what? He has.

Writing is the most horrible, awful, wonderful, awesome, godly experience I've had. And I can't take any credit for it. I can get arrogant with my speaking because God gave me those natural talents. But writing? Pfff! I got nothing. I have to totally rely on God to help bail me out. I feel guilty most of the time because that is my prayer—"God, bail me out again." And he has.

There are a couple of verses in the Bible that I hang on to.

> Brothers, think of what you were when you were called. Not many of you were wise by human standards; not many were influential; not many were of noble birth. But God chose the foolish things of the world to shame the wise; God chose the weak things of the world to shame the strong. He chose the lowly things of this world and the despised things—and the things that are not—to nullify the things that are, so that no one may boast before him. It is because of him that you are in Christ Jesus, who has become for us wisdom from God—that is, our righteousness, holiness and redemption. Therefore, as it is written: "Let him who boasts boast in the Lord."
>
> 1 Corinthians 1:26–31

> My message and my preaching were not with wise and persuasive words, but with a demonstration of the Spirit's power, so that your faith might not rest on men's wisdom, but on God's power.
>
> 1 Corinthians 2:4–5

I can't take any credit for my writing. My family laughs every time we get a new sales report. I have had four books on the CBA Teen Best-Seller list at one time, two books nominated for the Gold Medallion Award, and I'm the kid who can't read and write very good—I mean, very *well*. I just sit back and laugh and think, *Way to go, God. You're funny.*

Let this help motivate you. If you feel like God wants you to do something and it's something you're not great at, perfect! Go try it. You never know, God may want to use you to show off what it really means when 2 Corinthians 12:10 says, "That is why, for Christ's sake, I delight in weaknesses, in insults, in hardships, in persecutions, in difficulties. For when I am weak, then I am strong."

Nope. Hate 'em. They bore me. While some dude is sitting on their mama's couch playing video games about risk and adventure, I'm living it.

Hey, I'm not totally downing video games. If you use it for entertainment like going to the movies every once in a while, fine. But if that's all you do, then you need to get a life.

In John 10:10 Jesus says, "The thief comes only to steal and kill and destroy; I have come that they may have life, and have it to the full." I don't think he meant sitting around in your ergonomic-speaker-equipped gaming chair. I think he meant get up, get out, and live the adventure that others play video games about.

Did you know Justin and Emily love to country dance.

No, not line dancing, geek.

Subject: RE: #102 How do you write books if you can't read and write very well?

Date: Thursday, August 31, 2006 1:39 AM

From: Live conference

To: 'Justin Lookadoo' <emily@Lookadoo.com>

Conversation: The Universe at Large

Let me give you a rundown of how I go about writing a book.

1. I start by writing down as many ideas as I can.
2. Then I take out my yellow tablets and colored markers.
3. I begin writing about the issues.
4. I go back and fill in any blanks and complete any thoughts that I have.
5. I take what I wrote and type it into the computer.
6. I edit what I wrote.
7. I let someone else read it and make comments.
8. I go back and fix what needs to be corrected.
9. Finally I send it in.

Don't tell me you can't do something. It may take you a little longer and you may have to find a different way, but you can do it.

jlook

Justin Lookadoo
Buy Justin's hit new release **97**

Friday, March 2, 2007

#103 What is your take on global warming?

Yes, it's happening. That is proven. Could we as humans have an impact on it? I think it's entirely possible. Do I think humans are totally responsible for global warming? Well, not really.

If we are the total cause, how would you explain the global warming phenomenon on Mars? Yes, that is documented too. And I think the Martians already drive hybrid cars. That's not documented, but I'm pretty sure.

Now, I do "green" stuff. I recycle. I turn the lights off. I try not to eat food that gives me gas. Hey, don't laugh, methane gas can contribute. I think that is just a cool and responsible way to live and to show God that hey, I appreciate the world you gave me.

4:36 PM - **8 comments** - **5 Kudos** - **Add Comment**

Subject: RE: #104 What is the logarithmic binomial formula?
Date: Saturday, January 27, 2007 2:50 PM
From: Live conference
To: 'Justin Lookadoo' <emily@Lookadoo.com>
Conversation: The Universe at Large

I am glad you asked. First I must adjust your question slightly to read, "What is the logarithmic binomial *theorem*?" Now that we have that under control, I snicker, because a group of my scholarly friends and I were just discussing the probabilities of this being either true math or an Internet hoax. Either way, the formula is:

> But he said to me, "My grace is sufficient for you, for my power is made perfect in weakness." Therefore I will boast all the more gladly about my weaknesses, so that Christ's power may rest on me.
>
> 2 Corinthians 12:9

> Okay, this is funny. I actually found the logarithmic binomial theorem and was trying to figure out how to insert it. This verse was not it. The verse was just written there as a note, but I kinda like it like that. Who needs a logarithmic binomial theorem anyway?

jlook

Justin Lookadoo
See what is happening at www.Lookadoo.com

No. And I really don't think I have ADD. Oh, I don't care what the doctors and psychologists say. I think it's crap. I think most people like me who are "diagnosed" with it really don't have it. I think they may be hyper, maybe they have a short attention span, or maybe they just get bored easily. Whatever the deal, that doesn't mean I need a label and medication. With the huge amount of people in America with so-called ADD or ADHD, I think there is something wrong.

I don't want to take any meds for my so-called labeled condition. I have to be wired the way I am to do what I do. Sure, it makes writing harder, and I am sure I could pop some pill to make it easier, but why? I would lose that edge I have. That randomness is who I am. It's not an act or a show; it's who I am, so if you medicate me, you change who I am.

So how do I deal? I control what I eat. Not a lot of fast food crap, not a lot of sugar or other junk food. It's all pretty healthy stuff. I work out a lot. I control as much of the external stuff as I can. I control where I have to work. I can't have stuff everywhere. It has to be me alone at a clean desk, with no phone.

Control what you can and you will be amazed at your increased attention.

Lookadoo

Last Updated:
July 31, 2007

Send Message
Instant Message
Email to a Friend
Subscribe
Invite to My Blog

Gender: Male
Status: Married
Age: 101
Sign: Pisces

City: McKinney
State: TEXAS
Country: US

Signup Date:
02/17/06

Tuesday, March 13, 2007

#106 How do you feel about the technological advances of the twenty-first century and how do you think they will further advance in the next fifty years?

No comment.

4:50 PM - 6 comments - 2 Kudos - Add Comment

Subject: RE: #107 My parents are always in my biz.
How can I get them off my back?
Date: Monday, April 9, 2007 8:17 PM
From: Live conference
To: 'Justin Lookadoo' <emily@Lookadoo.com>
Conversation: The Universe at Large

Give them a bunch of info before they ask. Don't make them drag out all the details of your life. Tell them where you are going, when, why, and who you're going with, all before they ask anything. I can't give you any better answer than the one I put in *97: Random Thoughts about Life, Love, and Relationships*. Go grab that book and check out #94. It will explain everything.

That Looks Good

jlook

Attachment:

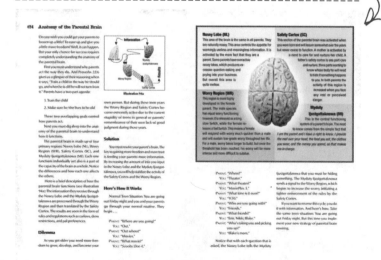

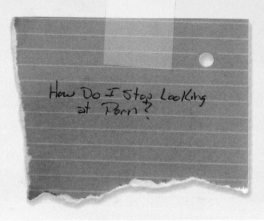

How Do I Stop Looking at Porn?

There are so many different levels of porn use, abuse, and addiction that it would take a while for me to go through everything. I think I'll write a book about that. But for now, let me give you some real stuff to do.

1. **Stop looking at it.** I know, duh! But when you feel the lust starting to flow, whether it's staring at a hottie or it's clicking the keys on the Internet, when you feel the urge, get up and walk away. Turn around and focus on something else. You have to break that cycle. You don't just wake up and look at porn. There's a process. You start by feeling this little urge to look at it. You try to fight it, but you go ahead and "check email." Then you do a little "searching" on the Internet. Then you move into thinking about looking. At some point during the whole process, *get up and walk away!*

2. **Don't surf solo.** Never ever be on your computer while you are alone. Sit at the kitchen table. If no one is home, wait until they get home. Leave the door open with your back to the door so you can't tell if someone is walking up behind you.

3. **Buddy up.** Get someone who you can count on. Tell them to ask you the tough questions about lust, porn, and masturbation. You have to be honest and answer them. Do this and keep doing this.

You have to get tough because the stuff you have tried doesn't seem to be working. Try something new and different. Do this and win.

Did you know Will Lane stayed with Justin and Emily all summer as an intern. If you don't know who Will is, check out the last chapter of 97.

Subject: RE: #109 What is the best way to say or show you are sorry?
Date: Wednesday, February 21, 2007 3:35 AM
From: Live conference
To: 'Justin Lookadoo' <emily@Lookadoo.com>
Conversation: The Universe at Large

Say it: "I'm sorry." Tell them why you are sorry and that you know what you did was hurtful, was disrespectful, and made them feel ugly, stupid, or whatever it made them feel.

Then change. Don't do it again. Be consistent in this. They may stay upset for a little while, and that's okay. But don't *you* get upset if they continue to be upset. That will blow away the sincerity of your apology.

jlook

Justin Lookadoo
Order your copy of the
3-part Dateable DVD now! *product@lookadoo.com*

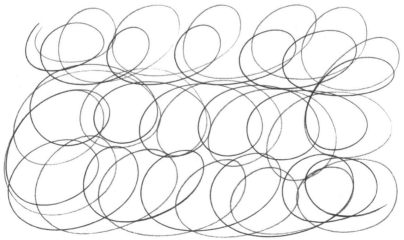

Lookadoo

Last Updated:
July 31, 2007

Send Message
Instant Message
Email to a Friend
Subscribe
Invite to My Blog

Gender: Male
Status: Married
Age: 101
Sign: Pisces

City: McKinney
State: TEXAS
Country: US

Signup Date:
02/17/06

Thursday, February 8, 2007

#110 What inspired you to become who you are today?

Wow, there have been so many influences and inspirations in my life. My mom inspired me to get up in front of people and speak. My dad inspired me to make this a career and not just a hobby. My sister pushed me to be funny when I watched her make people laugh. My wife inspired me to live what I say I believe. God's grace inspires me to forgive those who thrash me or the way I do things. Mr. House, my high school biology teacher, inspired me to get a biology degree. I spoke with a beautiful girl last week who is a junior in high school; she came up to me with tears in her eyes after a program and told me she wanted to change her relationship and her life. She inspired me to keep doing what I am doing.

2:10 AM - 2 comments - 15 Kudos - Add Comment

Did you know?

Emily and Justin dressed up like Pebbles and Bam-Bam at a costume party. He still hasn't gotten over the humiliation.

pictures have been burned . . . by accident.

As you can see

by the evidence in your hands, Justin writes some really cool books. But his first love is being face-to-face speaking to groups. He has done everything from small group interactions to huge music festivals to throwing down at an event at the House of Blues. He has done nearly 3,500 programs to about half a million people. He would love to come speak at your event. And his wife is always willing to send him out of the house. He is perfect for school programs, conferences, retreats, parenting conferences, staff development, and all kinds of leadership and special events. Check out what Justin can do for you at www .lookadoo.com or email him and Emily directly at speakers@ lookadoo.com. But definitely check out the website.

www.lookadoo.com

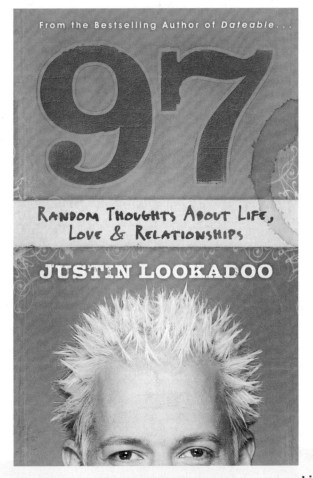

CAUTION:

These books are almost too hot to handle.

It's real. It's raw. It's true. **It's the Dirt.**

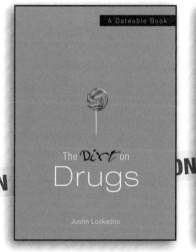

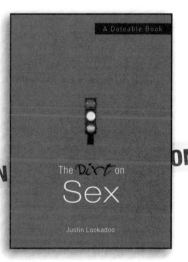